Born in Ballarat and raised in Derrinallum, Victoria, Sean O'Reilly qualified as a primary school teacher. At 23 he was virtually broke. By 33 he owned net assets of more than $1 million in shares and real estate, and a business that ran itself. After working hard and investing wisely, Sean never had to work again. He spends his time making and managing investments and enjoying life with his wife, Mary, and their three children, Zachary, Madison and Jackson.

Mairs Robson
17/9/01

ANYONE CAN BE A

Millionaire

SEAN O'REILLY

PAN
Pan Macmillan Australia

Acknowledgments

Without the help of so many people through the years this book would never have eventuated. There are so many people that I need to thank. You all know who you are.

I must give great thanks to my wonderful parents who always showed great confidence in us kids and taught us how to be so persistent through their own example.

Thanks to my eldest brother, Hugh, who initially introduced me to the idea of residential investment. To my financial advisor and accountant, Peter, who works so diligently and to my mentor, Tony, who always gave me his time. To Kevin Richardson, who helped me edit my manuscript initially. To Barb, who can type faster than I can think. To Sandra Porch from Landmark who led me in the right direction. To the team at Pan Macmillan for receiving my manuscript with such open arms and helping develop it to the stage that you now see.

I would like to thank the most important people in my life, my beautiful wife, Mary, and our three children, Zachary, Madison and Jackson, for their great support over the years. Over the last six months I've been writing they have had very little of my time. That will now change. Thank you all.

First published 2000 in Pan by Pan Macmillan Australia Pty Ltd
St Martins Tower, 31 Market Street, Sydney

Reprinted 2000

National Library of Australia
cataloguing-in-publication data:

O'Reilly, Sean, 1958 – .
Anyone can be a millionaire.

ISBN 0 330 36241 0.

1. Success in business. 2. Investments. I. Title.

650.1

The laws relating to superannuation, taxation, social security benefits, and the investment and handling of money, are constantly changing and may be subject to departmental discretion. While every care has been taken to ensure the accuracy of the material contained herein at the time of publication, neither the author nor the publisher will bear responsibility or liability for any action taken by any person, persons or organisations on the purported basis of information contained herein.

Without limiting the generality of the foregoing, no person, persons or organisation should invest monies or take other action on reliance of the material contained herein but instead should satisfy themselves independently (whether by expert advice or otherwise) on the appropriateness of any action.

Typeset in 11.5/15 pt Minion by Post Pre-Press Group, Brisbane
Printed in Australia by McPherson's Printing Group

CONTENTS

CONTENTS

INTRODUCTION

YOUR CHOICE – GO FOR BROKE...OR A MILLION

There are three kinds of people in this world: those who make things happen, those who watch things happen, and those who wonder what happened.

ANONYMOUS

At the age of 23, I was broke, my only possessions were a Holden Torana car worth about $1500 and $1000 in cash. Ten years later, I was a millionaire with net assets worth well over the million-dollar mark.

Many people believe that to become wealthy they need money behind them to get a start. Have you ever heard the comment 'You need money to make money', or 'His parents were rich, and they gave him a good start'?

There are also hundreds of thousands, perhaps millions, of Australians who put their hard-earned money into lottery tickets and watch the draw avidly on TV in the hope of becoming instant millionaires – even though the chance of winning a first division prize is as remote as one in eight million. Gambling of all types grew enormously during the 1990s. But it is well documented that many of those people who were lucky enough to land a windfall by winning large amounts in this manner are back where they started in less than five years.

People also believe that without a good education you can't become wealthy. Believe me, this is not the case at all. Many successful people left school early and have gone on to gain considerable wealth. I have a tertiary degree in education, but everything I learned in college and later went on to teach in schools has very little to do with the knowledge you need to become financially independent. Certainly, a college education set me up for the job which in turn brought in the income I needed to make my first investment. But even today, I know many teachers with the same or better college qualifications who struggle financially to get ahead. Worse still, many intensely dislike their jobs, but feel they must stick it out because they rely on the pay packet to live. These people have become slaves to their jobs.

Ask yourself: 'Does this describe me?' 'Do I believe I need money to make money?' 'Do I gamble?' 'Am I a slave to my job?' If your answer is 'yes' to any or all of these questions, then it leads to another even more important question: '*What am I going to do about it?*'

Let me give you some encouragement: you definitely do not need a windfall of money to get you going, and you won't have to rely on luck. Many Australians – including those famous people we all know about and others not so well known – have started with nothing and gone on to build their wealth, taking every opportunity to create for themselves a satisfying and rewarding lifestyle. I was one of these people, and for me, the gateway to wealth opened at a very early stage.

SMALL STEPS

When I was about 10 years old, I asked my mother for some pocket money, and she agreed to give me 10 cents a week; I wasn't actually handed the 10-cent coin, but I wrote down the amount each Sunday and added another 10 cents to my tally. Each time my pocket money grew to one dollar I was given the money to personally deposit into a bank account, which made a deep impression on me. Through some tough years growing up on the land, and later as an adult, that simple act strengthened my will to improve my own financial position.

As the middle child in a family of seven children, I had one vital thing going for me, and that was wonderful parents and the close-knit family they nurtured so well. We lived on a small farm in Victoria's Western District, with very little in the way of toys, pushbikes or the sort of material goods some families take for granted, and setting off for school with money in our pockets to spend at the canteen was a rare experience. But one thing we had in abundance – certainly far more important than material goods of any description – was the love and trust we received from Mum and Dad. Our closeness as a family has never changed; to this day I can't remember ever fighting with anyone in my family.

During my teenage years, the O'Reilly family fought fires, endured droughts, battled plagues of crickets and other pests as well as suffering disastrous wool prices, all of which exercised cruel control over the level of income my parents earned, even though my father was a very competent farmer. When I was in Form 2, about Year 8 in today's school system, I remember my Dad explaining to me why it was important to work hard, and to do well at school. I remember to this day the impression made on me by his advice – that I should seek a career which promised a far easier and more fulfilling course than the unpredictable ups and downs of his life on the land. The thought has stayed with me ever since; I had seen Dad do it hard and was determined to find an easier and hopefully more satisfying financial path than he experienced during his working life.

It was at about this time that my mind was made up – I was going to be a millionaire. When or how, I had no idea. Even the word 'millionaire' frightened me. I was on 10 cents a week at the time, which added up to a lot of weeks of saving to put together $1000 – actually, at 10 cents a week, it would take 192 years to reach $1000 . . . a long way from $1 million. Then something happened which gave me one of the best learning experiences of my life, although at the time I had no idea that it was a lesson in progress!

One freezing winter's morning the house cow we milked by hand each day had two very small twin calves. Unimpressed, the cow rejected her newborn calves, which then had only one hope for survival – to be bottle fed and cared for morning and night. Newborn calves were worth next to nothing, and when Dad came into the house and offered one each to my elder brother and me on condition that we looked after them, I jumped at the chance.

This calf was my first 'asset', and my head swam at the thought of the money I was about to make. I knew it would make far more money for me than my 10 cents per week. As Dad was an avid listener to the Stock and Land Market report on the radio each week, I knew that my calf, as a yearling, would sell for about $20. I worked out that receiving $20 for this calf in a year's time was the equivalent of being paid 10 cents a week for 200 weeks, or almost four years (200 weeks × 10 cents). To look at it another way, earning $20 in a single year amounted to 38 cents per week ($20 divided by 52 weeks), almost four times my weekly allowance from Mum. In other words, I had just increased my income by 380 per cent per week without a great increase in my workload. This led me to begin thinking laterally.

If Dad could be persuaded to give me another calf, I could double my income to about 760 per cent. He would say 'yes' wouldn't he? To my disappointment 'yes' was not the answer he gave. I had to find another way of increasing my income.

If your first idea doesn't work try another, and I certainly was not yet out of ideas. I offered to buy Dad's 10 old hens and sell him the eggs. He agreed to sell the hens for $1 each, and to pay me one cent per egg. I assumed each hen would lay one egg a day, and that within 100 days I would have my money back. Much to my disappointment, these old hens did not have one egg a day left in them, so it took a lot longer than 100 days to get my money back.

I then bought six young chickens for what seemed like a

huge amount, $3 each, but since they laid far more eggs, I recovered my investment much more rapidly. Business picked up when the local hotel offered to pay 50 cents for a dozen eggs, which – as I quickly calculated – was four times the price being paid to me by Dad.

This put me in a very difficult position. As a keen businessman I wanted to sell all of my eggs to the hotel, but could only do so after my mother took enough for our own household. Since my profits were now at stake, I promptly gave up asking for eggs at breakfast time! My fledgling egg business was now returning about $1 a week, which seemed (and was) a lot of money to me at the time. After all, I had begun on 10 cents a week and had progressed quickly to $1.10 a week. This is no less than an increase of 1000 per cent (10 cents × 1000 per cent).

You are now probably asking what does 10 cents × 1000 per cent = $1.10 have to do with becoming a millionaire? My answer to that question is: a lot.

The 10 cents I was initially being paid was my starting wage and, no matter how hard I worked at home doing the chores around the house, I could still hope for no more pay than the agreed 10 cents. Today, many young people start out in full-time jobs on wages of, say, $20,000 a year. No matter how hard they work in their 38 hours a week they still receive no more than $20,000. Standing beside them may be a fellow employee who works at half their pace but who will also be paid $20,000 a year. Is this fair? Most people will have experienced this situation and many would agree it isn't fair.

For most people, the only way to increase their income

and improve their standard of living is to obtain a pay rise. I see so many people who have advanced as far as they ever will in their jobs. They have absolutely no avenue for further advancement. Worse, they constantly have to ask (or beg) their employer for pay rises. Of course, the employer can only provide jobs (and pay rises) if a profit can be made from the employee's labour. If your pay rise is likely to wipe out the business profit, the request won't even be considered – nor is it ever easy to convince the boss that he makes enough profit from your work to justify paying you more.

It's true that those who reach a dead-end in their jobs can resign and find work elsewhere, but even then, when the excitement of a new challenge wears off after a couple of years, the old feelings of being unfairly treated or paid less than you are worth return. Are you really any better off than you were in the previous job?

This brings me back to a point I raised earlier. If you answered 'yes' to those questions I posed earlier, then you do need to decide what you intend to do about it. In just about every case, the freedom of movement you are looking for will involve improving your financial situation.

THE AIM OF THIS BOOK

Those who follow the universal principles underlying wealth creation and success in life create the conditions for a richer and more satisfying future. Almost anyone born in a free and prosperous country such as Australia has the ability and the means to become a millionaire. I sincerely believe that this book can help you develop the long-term strategic financial plan you've been dreaming about to set yourself up for the rest of your life.

There are two major ways of increasing your income, and both involve leveraging. You can leverage either your time, or you can leverage your money, two methods that are discussed in detail throughout this book. To leverage your time you must start some form of business selling a service, such as cleaning, plumbing, or tutoring, just to mention a few; or dealing with some product, either at the manufacturing, wholesale or retail level. To leverage your money you must save and invest, setting yourself up for the wise use of borrowed money to invest in more assets such as shares and real estate, or in the buying or building of other businesses.

For every parent reading this book there is a bonus – learning the lessons of these chapters will not only be to your own benefit, but will help you teach your own children to make an early start on the road to achieving financial independence. Age does not matter; you are never too old nor too young to begin investing. Actually, I believe everyone should be investing throughout their entire lives, and the goal of financial independence is far easier to attain if you start at an early age.

Financial independence or financial success represents different degrees of net worth for different people. It might be the ability to tell your boss you no longer need to work for him/her or anyone else. Perhaps you have paid out your mortgage and have no loans or credit card debt, but you remain sufficiently concerned about your future to look for a plan to improve your situation. Maybe, despite getting regular pay rises and promotions, there never seems to be any money left at the end of your week. Get the message? You can achieve the degree of financial success you want.

I don't claim that it will be at all easy or that it will happen quickly, but there is no doubt that you *can* make the grade if you are willing to put in the time and the hard work. This will involve giving up many of the things you love doing now so that you can reap rich rewards down the track.

There is no magic formula and there are no secrets about wealth that have not already been available to you previously. I gathered everything I required to help me succeed by asking questions, reading many books, listening to many tapes and by making many, many mistakes, in the full knowledge that each mistake was a necessary companion along my road to financial independence. My main source of information was from those who went before me, and their main source of information was almost certainly from people who had also 'been there and done that'. I am not reinventing the wheel but I might be putting my own spoke into this particular wheel every now and then.

It has been estimated that about one in every hundred people will become a millionaire in Australia, which suggests there could be as many as 190,000 reaching that status at some time. You can be part of that group, the choice is up to you.

We all have experienced and benefited from much the same education system, yet most people have a lot of trouble making the amount of money they need to buy the things they want. On reaching retirement, most people have no choice but to accept a government's pension, while only a few others have sufficient money to go where they wish and to buy what they want.

It's interesting how often those who excel in any area of life are seen as 'lucky'. The truth is that, in almost every such case, these successful people have created their own 'luck' by actively looking for opportunities and virtually hunting them down. Rather than put their achievements down to luck, I suggest we face the truth – these people thoroughly earn their success.

I did not win Tattslotto, nor did my assets come down to me through inheritance. I worked very hard; determined never to give up on the 'big picture', and I set clear goals and worked toward them one step at a time. My success has been the outcome of a continual process of learning, and I say very confidently that if you take up the challenge, so will yours.

I am willing to share everything I have learned with every confidence that it can help you in some way. But don't accept everything in this book as an instruction to be followed to the letter – keep your mind open. I must make it very clear to you that I am not a financial planner or an accountant and have no qualifications in these areas. Most of what I have learned I have learned from 'walking the walk' and not just 'talking the talk'. Certainly, I would strongly advise anyone interested in moving into any field of investment to engage the services of at least one financial adviser. Use my experience and examples as a guide to ways which can help in your particular circumstances.

When I was 23 and a primary school teacher, the idea of spending the next 35 years of my life, or more, stuck in the same job without enough money at the end of the week to give me the lifestyle I wanted, had no appeal at all. Determined to do something about it, I quickly worked out that changing my financial situation demanded that I try something totally different. If you want to see where you will be in 10 years time, take a look at where you have come from over the past 10 years, and if you're not happy with your progress, get the message – your approach needs to change drastically.

That is no easy decision; habits picked up over a decade are difficult to change. But, make the decision. Set the goal that clearly pinpoints where you want to be in 10 years' time and let me help you get there. I assure you the choice is entirely yours and you really can have anything you want so long as you are willing to work hard for it.

You were born to succeed, which is not the same as saying it will be easy. In fact, it will require continuous hard work, but the achievement is well worth it. At the age of 34, I was what I would call financially free, knowing that I never had to actively work in a paid job again because my investments produced more than enough to live on. That doesn't mean that I am inactive; I actually put a great deal of effort and time into those business and personal pursuits which I most enjoy. However, it is a great feeling to know that I don't have to go in to work tomorrow, and that I have the freedom to holiday wherever and whenever I choose.

I know this book will help you as it takes you through the steps and skills required for successful investing in property and shares; choosing an adviser, using banks to your advantage, minimising tax and understanding many investment strategies. An essential objective of this book is to show you how to get assets working for you to establish a passive income capable of replacing your active, work-related income forever.

HOW TO GET THE MOST OUT OF THIS BOOK

The people who will get the most from this book are those with a deep desire to learn and the determination to manage money better and build wealth for the benefit of themselves and their families. If that means you, constantly remind yourself how important these principles are to you, and picture yourself gaining the mastery of your affairs which will lead to a richer, fuller, happier and more fulfilling life.

- Stop frequently in your reading to think over what you are reading. Ask yourself just how and when you can apply each suggestion to your own particular situation.
- Use a highlighter pen to highlight those points you think are most relevant.
- Draw, write and scribble all over this book; marking and underscoring a book makes it more interesting – and much easier to review rapidly. Most people think better with pencil in hand; writing down ideas focuses our full attention on them. It's also a good idea to keep pencil and pad beside the bed to make note of new ideas which emerge during those waking periods at night when so

many good ideas are generated. How often we forget them by the time the sun rises.

➡ Constantly remind yourself of the importance of being financially free; released from the slavery of financial dependence. Convince yourself of the benefits and pleasures of being master of your own time and destiny.

➡ If you seek real, lasting benefit from this book, don't imagine that skimming through once will be enough. After reading it thoroughly, spend a few hours reviewing it every month. Keep it on the desk in front of you every day.

Remember that use of the principles outlined in this book will become habit only by constantly and consciously putting them to use. There is no other way. Learning is an active process. We learn by doing. So, to master the principles you will be studying in this book, be quick to do something about them. Apply them at the earliest and every opportunity, remembering that if you don't, you will forget them quickly. Only knowledge that is used sticks in the memory.

This book is not about merely gaining information. In reading it you are showing a willingness to form new habits. You are attempting a new way of life, and that will require time, persistence and daily application. Have your spouse or partner read the book as well. The attitudes of those involved with you in the quest for financial independence is extremely important; their complete support and understanding is essential.

Reading the book may sometimes seem something of a

grind, but it need not be. One of the keys to the art of staying with a task is in knowing how and when to back off for a while. Blind perseverance is for fools. It involves working harder rather than smarter and, let's face it, it is often smart when facing a mental blockage to make a tactical retreat for a while, by going for a walk, for example. This will allow more time to take in and digest information. Take the time. It will be well worth it.

Congratulations – you have already taken the first step toward your goals by reading this book. You are on your way to becoming a millionaire. Take one small step at a time and the road won't be nearly as difficult as you perhaps once thought.

PART 1

Financially Free

1

WHAT IS FINANCIAL
INDEPENDENCE?

The term 'financial independence' has a grand ring to it. But it has a very simple meaning, although we all may have our own ways of expressing what it actually means to us. For most people it will be financial freedom or financial success, but financial independence has different degrees of net value for different individuals. I reached a state of financial independence when I knew that I had enough 'passive' income to give up the active work I previously had to do to bring in my regular wage, or 'active' income. Passive income is the income flowing from investments such as shares, property and interest on cash deposits; income that doesn't require my personal exertion as an employee in a regular job.

And that's what it's really all about; financial independence gives you choices – the choice to do your own thing every day and the choice to buy what you want, when you want. It gives you freedom from the petty problems of life; those 'big' little things of daily life such as the car repayment, the grocery bill, the child's new school shoes and unexpected expenses. These are problems we all have faced at some time, but – believe me – they are far less worrying, frustrating or difficult when you have the money to cover them. You can even buy that dream house you saw in the magazine; for once, it's up to you.

In other ways too, financial independence frees us from doing the things we dislike, or – to look at it in a more positive sense – it provides the freedom to do what we really want with our lives. Instead of washing the car or cleaning the house, why not employ someone who wants the work to provide them with their active income? If it suits your lifestyle, go to a restaurant more often instead of spending time in the kitchen at home. Financial independence makes you your own boss.

Without financial independence we can become slaves to our jobs, and that all too often leaves us with the awful problem of struggling to provide the lifestyle, security and, yes, dignity that we hoped for in our old age. Planning for your financial future after retirement can be a worrying task. Will you be able to live on the pension alone when you retire? The pension is about one-third of average weekly earnings, barely enough to provide the basic necessities of life. That would be about $8000 a year.

And, of course, if you are a parent, financial independence is not only of importance to you – your whole family has a huge stake in the overall financial situation, good or bad. Financial independence can do good things for your spouse and children. It can relieve the marriage of financial conflict, which counsellors say is one of the primary causes of marital conflict. It will allow you to provide adequately for the emotional, material and educational needs of your children; the cost of their education, for example, has become quite enormous and beyond the means of many families.

Making provision for family needs involves many parents in working longer hours, and they often fall into the trap of borrowing to satisfy their own and their children's craving for the current 'in thing'. Then they have to work even longer hours to pay off debt, digging for themselves an even deeper hole which will eventually cave in on them. And as children grow so quickly many parents end up wondering where the years went. There certainly is a need to spend quality time with our children while we can, but we must also spend quantity time with them.

In the longer term, financial independence enables you to be a role model for others in the family, instilling in them the proper understanding of money and financial success. Most people want it now, and most people will get it now – the large TV set to replace the perfectly good model they already own, or the new car they bought (because their best friend has just bought one) even though the current car is only five years old, is just as safe and just as reliable. But watching you save money now and doing without the little things in life so that you can have what you want later on is a great lesson for your children.

Financial independence also gives you the ability to donate money to any organisation you wish to support, your church, school, local community organisation, or to an overseas humanitarian aid group. The choice becomes yours, and the wealth you gain can bring great benefit to many others.

For anyone genuinely interested in building wealth, you must learn to do without the things that bring instant gratification but are not necessary now, so that you can build wealth. That takes patience, a lot of it – becoming wealthy won't happen overnight, but you can begin on the road to financial freedom today. What better time to start? Some people will make staggering strides in a matter of years; others will take 10 years to achieve their goals, while others will take 20 and more. The good thing is that it doesn't really matter how long it takes, provided you begin on the road today, or have already begun the journey.

Many people on excellent incomes spend it all on day-to-day living, confident they will make it back tomorrow in their 'very secure job'. But in the face of the heavy downsizing policies of many large companies throughout the past decade, a process which shows no signs of slowing, just how secure is your job? Will it be there tomorrow? Of course, the answer is that most jobs are not at all secure. Downsizing, changes in company policy and takeovers and mergers are all threats to job security, nor can we be certain that the company we work for won't go bankrupt tomorrow. Let's face it, if the company is heading that way, the employee will be among the last to know. Redundancy payouts to those unfortunate enough to lose their jobs are often spent quickly. And when new jobs turn up, the pay packet is usually far less generous than before. The self-employed contractor and small business person often mistakenly see their situations as secure, when the reality is that the arrival of strong competition could cost them half their customers, perhaps driving them to a loss if they continue trading. It is a common enough situation, in which overspending and too little careful investing during the good years leaves too little money to survive on when those contracts no longer come in.

Even people with high incomes often confuse this with wealth. A person earning $100,000 a year is on a top income, but may not be wealthy. How long could they survive if they lost or gave up their work tomorrow? The wise ones with good investments would survive, but many high income earners would have trouble covering all of their ongoing debts by the end of the month. We all know the type likely to be in strife. At the head of the list would be the buyer who spends everything on the better car, the bigger house (with a bigger mortgage), the new fashions, or eats at the top restaurants. What would they do if their partner asked them to go overseas for, say, six months? Will they survive financially? Would you survive?

Let's look at the phrase again: 'will you survive?'.

Thousands of Australians live 'on the edge of broke' for their entire lives, and it's fair to wonder what this does to their mental and emotional state, and to their physical condition. I wonder how many years we can subtract from the average life of someone who is always stressed thinking about how to pay off the next bill. This must surely be a major factor in many health disorders. Do you have ulcers and are you sleeping well? But let's be positive and assume that, whatever the state of your health or your wallet, you do want to improve your position and set out to obtain true financial freedom. In that case, learn and follow the rules of the game, which are fairly simple.

THE RULES

→ Motivate yourself to take that vital first step toward becoming a millionaire. No one else will do it for you.

→ Use the negative views of people who tell you it is not possible to become financially free as a motivating force. By facing and working around setbacks along the way, prove to them that they are wrong.

→ Start early, but reject the idea that you have to be 55 years of age before you can retire. You can retire at any age you choose.

→ Decide on the $ value which for you represents financial independence. Don't set your sights too low.

→ Budget compulsively. Don't be at all worried about what other people think.

→ Be willing to learn, and – enjoy it.

And remember – most of the wealthy people of today started out just like you, with very basic incomes. The difference is that they *planned* to become wealthy. Just like building a house they began with a plan; stuck to its broad outlines throughout but importantly, changed many of the details as circumstances required along the way. They just kept plugging along, one brick at a time. When problems were encountered, such as the soil test which shattered their hopes of building the house as initially planned, they worked around the problem. They didn't give up. They never stopped building.

Among those on today's wealthy lists are people still earning only average active incomes, which underlines a point of crucial importance. Whether or not you are wealthy does not have anything to do with what sort of income you earn. It's not what you get paid but what you do with the money that counts.

An early step toward building wealth is the listing and valuing of net assets, to determine your actual worth. There is an old saying which makes the point well:

Wealthy people invest first and spend the rest.
Poor people spend first and invest the rest.

The message is – look after your investments first.

2

THINK LIKE A MILLIONAIRE

Why is it that as children we have fabulous dreams about what we will do and be as adults, but as we become older our dreams go out the door? Is it because someone has told us to stop dreaming and just get on with our lives? Now, you're probably asking what has any of this to do with becoming a millionaire. Why am I not just telling you how to buy shares and property so that you can get on with making money? Knowing how to buy shares and property is all very well, but without genuine belief in yourself the chances of you becoming a millionaire are very small. Understanding how the people who become millionaires think is critical to your chances of making the grade.

Childhood dreams, in my opinion, can have lasting effects upon our lives. In a way, dreaming of financial independence is something like those childhood dreams, and they require encouragement and nurturing if you are to develop the right positive attitude.

If you believe that you will never be a millionaire then

you are correct, but on the other hand, if you believe that you will be a millionaire then you also are likely to be correct. You may have heard this quote before:

If you think you can or if you think you can't, then you are right.

Reread it and ponder on it. Write it down and stick it someplace where you will see it daily. It will help you think like a millionaire.

As an individual, you have to believe that you can become a millionaire. This leads you to the conviction that your quest will succeed and sufficient faith in your own capacity to *know* that 'Yes, I will be a millionaire'. Belief in one's ability to succeed is the one basic, absolutely essential ingredient in the story of all successful people; if you believe, really believe you can succeed, you will. Even if at the outset you don't have great confidence that you can ever become a millionaire, don't lose heart. You can awaken within yourself the drive to follow your dream, and with it the belief that you will become a millionaire. Then run with it.

Here are some strategies to help you think like a millionaire.

FORGET THE PAST

Don't look back on past experience and assume that your future will be more of the same, nor should you waste time and energy fretting over previous mistakes and missed opportunities. You can't alter the past, it has gone – but you can learn from it. Use its lessons to help control your present and future actions, with the focus on positive ideas. It is a fact that your belief (or lack of it) in your own potential will have a huge bearing on the success or failure patterns that mark your passage through life. Where you are today is all your own work, and it is important to appreciate that what you think, feel and believe today is playing a big role in shaping what happens in your life tomorrow.

Begin right away by raising the level of your goals; if you think small, then your achievements will be small, but think big and your successes will be correspondingly greater. Attitude is crucial in anything we do. We are a product of our own thoughts.

Most of us live with doubts about our own abilities, allowing negative forces to get in our way. Once in the mind, however, unfounded negativity can be a powerful influence, one which we ourselves unfortunately encourage by our own lack of belief. When you don't fully believe in what you are doing your mind will attract reasons to support any area of disbelief, a feature of most of our failed efforts. If you think uncertainty, you will fail. If you think victory, you will succeed.

A strong belief in a successful outcome will set the mind to figuring out ways and means of actually achieving the victory. The 'how-to-do-it' will always come to the person who believes that 'he-can-do-it'. No person has achieved anything worthwhile without developing a strong belief in themselves. When you believe something long enough and hard enough your beliefs will come through.

Attitudes of a Millionaire What is it that makes certain people become millionaires? How is it that some people seem to rise above the crowd to greater levels of achievement than others?

The attitude of 'I can't do it' is defeated even before it begins. Simply changing your attitude can trigger enormous changes in your life. Positive changes come with positive attitudes.

The millionaire does few things that cannot be done by the average person. He or she is just like you and me.

What millionaires do have is a positive attitude, and the clear message for anyone who really wants to succeed, is that a creative positive attitude is a must. Visualise yourself as a winner.

Believe in your possibilities and disbelieve your doubts. Never see yourself as a victim of circumstances, but instead as one in control of the environment in which you operate. Don't look behind you in life; focus on the future.

We encounter many challenges, setbacks and victories in our daily lives, and we must take personal responsibility for all of them, resisting the temptation to blame others as things go wrong from time to time.

It is also helpful to look on our mistakes we all inevitably make as learning experiences rather than failures.

And you might have spent a lot of time and effort convincing yourself it is impossible to achieve your goal, a thought you must replace with the proposition that 'It is very possible to become a millionaire'.

My wife, Mary, and I had tremendous desire to become financially free and to win each battle along the way. The level of our desire and the passionate pursuit of the goal of financial independence sustained and focused our attention on what was required to succeed. The quest for financial freedom needs that kind of motivation, continually applied, if you are to be successful; there is no point in getting all worked up about it on New Year's Eve if the thought disappears as soon as you return to work.

You must desire money. You must think money. You must develop a definite money-making instinct. Become money orientated and this special attitude of mind will attract wealth to you. Acquiring money is a talent that definitely can be learned, although I should stress that I am not advising anyone to chase money for money's sake. Don't look upon money simply as dollars and cents, but as a vehicle which will help you achieve your lifelong dreams.

ENTHUSIASM

Along with a positive attitude, the successful individual must have great enthusiasm. A basic element of success, enthusiasm flows from a sense of commitment and confidence in the ability to achieve goals. Confidence can be boosted by 'seeing' yourself on the verge of becoming financially free, by visualising yourself in that position. Enthusiasm will ensure that you never give up, despite any obstacle. It holds negative thoughts at bay and keeps the mind from even stray thoughts about giving up the struggle.

To get your enthusiasm level up, sit in the car of your

dreams, visit the house you hardly dared dream about and study those brochures of an exotic paradise. Or imagine that every morning is like your dream Sunday morning – sleeping in or enjoying breakfast at whatever time and in whatever style suits your fancy. Pretend you are already a millionaire, and financially free.

SELF-TALK

Another way to convince yourself that 'You can if you think you can' is to use the powers of self-talk, repeating a phrase over and over again to yourself. It works like this. With repetition, an idea will gradually be accepted by your subconscious, and the mind comes to believe in that idea as it is repeated over and over. Eventually, your actions will reflect that belief.

The secret to developing this belief rests in words, combined with images, which are linked with the special way in which thoughts express themselves. Merely repeating a phrase is of no use unless feeling is mixed with the words, since our subconscious minds recognise and act only upon thoughts that reflect our emotions.

At an early stage in my self-development I used to repeat to myself:

I will be a millionaire.

I will be a millionaire.

After repeating the message many, many times I truly believed it, changing the message as I came closer to my goal to:

I am a millionaire.

I am a millionaire.

Actually, I didn't have $1,000,000 worth of net assets at this time, but I could already 'see' myself having it, and repetition of the phrase reinforced the strength of that feeling.

Let's look at self-talk from a different angle. I know the concept is difficult to accept when explained for the first time. Assume that we have a big day ahead of us tomorrow, and we already see some obstacles which will make it a lot more difficult than we would like. The self-talk we might repeat for this occasion will be something like:

Tomorrow will be so productive that I will get everything done.

Tomorrow will be so productive that I will get everything done.

By tomorrow, the phrase becomes:

Today will be so productive that I will get everything done.

Today will be so productive that I will get everything done.

Guess what the outcomes of the day will be – but don't take my word for it, test it out on any small thing. All I ask is that you make it a fair test by giving it time to work, and plenty of enthusiasm.

THE SUBCONSCIOUS MIND

Most of us are aware that our subconscious minds are controlled by the imagination. I wonder how many are aware that the subconscious is far more powerful than the conscious part of our minds. When we think we can't do something it is usually our vast imagination which is controlling our thoughts and actions.

The conscious mind, with its message of 'you can do it', is often fighting a losing battle with your imagination. For example, why don't many more people go bungee jumping when it is supposed to be so much 'fun'? Although we may know that the jump is quite safe and well regulated, our imaginations still run wild.

Well, if your subconscious mind and its imaginings can sometimes prevent you doing something, why can't it also talk you into actually doing something on other occasions? The answer is that it can, and that if you feed your imagination with positive images they will set the stage for you to take that constructive step forward. Say it again, and again:

I will be a millionaire.

Without our realising it, our past experiences and our imagination often convince us that we simply aren't the type of person who could ever become a millionaire, whether or not we have the qualities needed to do just that.

External circumstances end up matching the image you have of yourself with amazing accuracy, with positive or very negative results depending on individual attitudes.

For self-talk to work for you, you have to use it, repeat

your message over and over again. Words and language play a major role in our lives and therefore have tremendous power. When you decide to use the right words to your advantage through self-talk, expect to be amazed at their range and power.

HOW MUCH ARE YOU WORTH?

Some people are paid $15 an hour; others $50, $100 or even $300 an hour. Take a look at your own situation – what are you paid for each hour, what would you like to be paid, and what do you think you are worth?

Before responding to those questions, you also need to work out whether you give value for money and work as hard as others you know. Only then should you consider why the amount you receive for each hour of work is so far below the hourly rate of others. It may have something to do with the value you actually place on yourself. If you think you are worth $40 an hour, then go out and find the job or business that will give you that sort of return. Don't undervalue yourself; we all have the right to seek payment at the rate which matches the quality of our work, rather than merely accepting what someone else thinks we are worth.

The level at which you are now being paid means much more than you think. In fact, your pay represents almost to the cent how you value yourself as a person. Let's look at it in a different way. Many people believe they will always have a mortgage and that when they retire at the age of 60 they will depend on a pension. While you think this way, so shall it be, but if you think you are going to be a millionaire and will retire in 10, 15 or 20 years, again, so shall it be.

The events in your life are a mirror image of your thoughts. All high achievers firmly believe they can accomplish great things. Similarly, all those who will become rich are deeply convinced that they will some day be rich. That's why they succeed.

I have always been fascinated to see how closely the level of salary paid or contract fee received actually reflects a person's view of his own worth. It is in direct proportion to self-image, which in so many instances is the cause of dissatisfaction. The mental limitations we impose on ourselves will perfectly match the limits we encounter in life. It's a case of direct cause and effect. Therefore, if we strive for higher income and greater recognition at work or business, we must first improve our self-image, a process which itself has no limits if we tackle it with energy and conviction.

One way to create and maintain a healthy self-image is to associate with positive people who themselves have great personal confidence. They will give you positive recognition and feedback, which in turn adds to your own sense of worth and expands the ego. A strong ego, preferably one well under control is one of your most valued assets.

Negative people are all too ready to knock you down but very few are willing to pick you up – that responsibility remains yours, and yours alone. Away from the workplace, family and friends close to you are going to hook you emotionally. Train and encourage them to do that in a positive way.

PRODUCTIVITY

Self-image and productivity share a very close relationship. Get out of bed feeling great about yourself in the morning and you will turn in a productive effort during that day. I begin each day with the thought, 'Every day I will improve', and – as a believer in self-talk – I often say this sentence to myself and repeat it aloud.

Like everything else worthwhile in life, building of self-esteem demands conscious effort. Education has a big role to play, and I don't mean in a narrow sense, such as doing well at school, university or some other form of tertiary study. Your education might include quite different interests you enjoy, such as physical fitness, cooking, dress sense or public speaking. Learning anything at all is good for us, but doing well at something we really believe in – and sharing that learning with other positive people we like – is always a plus for personal self-esteem.

It would be difficult to over-emphasise the importance of self-esteem, since those who have it in big doses usually do better in family relations, business, jobs, finance and hobbies, while the opposite is generally true of people with low self-esteem. They tend to see success simply in materialistic terms; thus, 'the more possessions you own the more successful you are'. Since low self-esteem often leads to high levels of physical and emotional stress, as well as high absentee rates, little wonder this group suffers from lower productivity.

PROMOTE YOURSELF

Picture this. Your work performance is excellent and yet you might as well be completely invisible in your workplace. But, make one mistake and the roof falls in, with bosses, colleagues and others just waiting to pounce. It's sad, but it happens so often – and we contribute to it ourselves by our failure to promote ourselves in our day-to-day performance. Rather than give ourselves a pat on the back for the good things we do, we focus on those that go wrong, picking ourselves to pieces for those little mistakes. We all have reasons to congratulate ourselves on aspects of our performance and the positive attributes that make us valuable members of a group or team, and we should not hesitate to grab every opportunity. Feeling good about yourself is not a luxury; it is an absolute necessity.

Try writing down the things you do well and give you a sense of pride. Read through the list each morning, as you sit down for breakfast. Add or delete items from time to time, but always express your thoughts in a very positive manner. For example, I Am Proud of Myself Because:

I am always very punctual.

I am always very polite and treat others as I would like to be treated.

I very diligently maintain a budget, recording every cent I spend.

I am very good at reading self-improvement books.

I maintain an accurate and detailed diary.

Include anything that gives you a sense of pride. Done properly, it can help identify overall strengths and positive personal qualities which, when clearly understood, can give a greater sense of direction, increased confidence and higher self-esteem. People who feel good about themselves produce positive results.

We shouldn't be shy about calling attention to our abilities and achievements. We don't hesitate to praise particular skills or qualities in others when in truth our own qualities are just as deserving but not fully recognised, even by ourselves. Successful people don't hide their achievements, and neither should you. They intensify their own images by self-promotion, and getting a feel for self-promotion could also help you.

Honestly complimenting other people on their efforts can strengthen our own thoughts about ourselves. While we must initially accept ourselves as we are while working on self-improvement, it is important to know and take pride in our good points. Get into the habit of providing frequent and positive reinforcement within your own family and circle of friends. It will be good for them and it will also help to reinforce your own actions. But keep self-promotion in perspective, don't overdo it.

KEEP GROWING

Many people will simply 'Go through life', while others adopt the position that they will 'Grow through life', a philosophy I certainly follow. There are those in their 30s and 40s who dislike immensely the jobs they do but are still willing to continue in that job for the next 10, 20 or 30 years – not much of a life, in my opinion.

Personal growth requires that we continually learn new things. The person who does not learn or push the boundaries of his/her knowledge will go backwards. A 'good effort', should not satisfy you unless that 'good effort', is getting better every day. The actual level of your earlier accomplishment doesn't really matter; while you continue to grow in personal terms your life will get better and better. The quickest way to age is to become bored with life and to stop learning. Be an enthusiast and keep educating yourself.

BE LOYAL TO YOURSELF

Loyalty is a quality prized in every avenue of life, yet it strikes me that although there is no doubt about our loyalty to others we often let ourselves down. We must always be loyal to ourselves, never giving up on ourselves, even in the face of small or large problems or when we have made the inevitable mistake. Every mistake is just another learning experience. You never fail, nor should you look on your mistakes as 'failures'. The only failure is to give up the fight; if you lack the will to try again or to tackle the issue in a different way, then you certainly have failed.

A failure is not a person. It is an event. Trust yourself to achieve a particular goal, even though not everything you do will be completely successful. Recognise problems as they arise but press on to face and overcome every challenge that may arise. One mark of the top performer is willingness to go that extra mile, and to do the extra thing.

KEEP IT NICE

My parents had a saying which made a big impression on me as a young man: 'If you don't have something nice to say about someone, don't say anything at all'. I was slow to realise at the time that this applied to my inner thoughts about myself as well.

If you have nothing nice to say about yourself, and only negative thoughts come to mind, then 'don't say anything at all'. As bad thoughts about yourself make their presence felt, get rid of them. And try to do the same in wider society, where there is no shortage of bad thoughts and negative thinking. Never condone gossip by remaining to listen; get out of there fast. It shows strength of character. When you sling mud you do nothing more than lose ground.

3

STARTING NOW

How many people have said they wished they had done something or other when they were 'a lot younger'? My reply to that is simple and to the point: You are never too old to do anything; you are exactly as young as you think. There is an impression in our society that serious ageing kicks in during a person's early fifties, with the body and mind falling apart rapidly from then on. This, of course, is not the case at all, and it's an important myth to explode. Ray Crock, for example, was in his fifties when he opened the first McDonald's restaurant. Many, perhaps most people, might think that they're too old to begin investing. You are never too old to begin, and no matter the form of investment you choose, it is possible to make your retirement lifestyle so much better. Old is a relative term.

Up to a certain point your real age is determined less by your biological clock than by the way you think, act and feel, and there is no reason why advancing years or previous setbacks alone should prevent anyone achieving the goal of becoming financially free. For those who doubt this, it must come as a surprise to realise that almost half of the top executives in any country are between the ages of 55 and 90 years. American car-industry pioneer, Henry Ford, certainly understood the value of maturity. He maintained that if all the experience and judgment of men over the age of 50 was to disappear there wouldn't be enough of either left to run the world.

But don't get me wrong; while I am arguing that it is never too late to start, there is no doubt that the younger you begin investing the easier it is, and by a long way. The biggest advantage the young starters have over anyone else involved in investing is that they have time on their side. They can achieve financial independence without the need to work miracles, without taking undue risks, and without the unlikely ingredient of extraordinarily good luck.

So, when should we become involved in investments? In my view, investing has a place for children from the time they can recognise the value of money, probably during early years in primary school.

CHILDREN AND FINANCE

All parents have responsibilities toward their children, ranging from helping them develop their own set of positive values to learning the various social skills they require, and – just as importantly – teaching them to become successful in finance. But how can we prepare our children and provide the skills necessary for them to become financially free later in life? How much guiding and shaping should our children be given if they are to lead successful lives?

All too often, when we set specific early goals for our children, we lead them instead to frustration and failure. Don't tell your children what their goals should be. Don't tell them they must have a good education and a great job with a high income. Trying to persuade our children to go down some particular path (sometimes because it appeals to our own egos) won't necessarily lead them to success and happiness.

Parents naturally like to shield their children from the mistakes they or others have made, and it is understandable that they hope their children will 'do better than we did'. However, if this means the child cannot make his or her own mistakes then no real learning takes place. There is no freedom for them at all. Children must play their own 'game of life', and that means experimenting, learning to win. In every game there will be 'winners' and 'losers', although I prefer to see it as 'winners' and 'learners'.

Play different games, such as Monopoly, draughts, cards and chess, with your children. (After all, later in this book – and in life itself – you will be playing a sort of Monopoly but buying the houses with real money.) Toys and games help children develop their creative and problem-solving talents, and every child loves playing games.

Financial independence is a game. People who struggle financially can't lay the blame on their inability to earn enough money, they struggle because they haven't learned the game of finance – they don't know what to do with their money once they get it. Therefore don't guide your children by telling them to do what you would do. Let them make up their own minds; ask questions to stimulate discussion, like:

What are you going to do next?

Well, I think I am going to do this.

Good idea. How do you plan to do that?

The child who makes his own decisions knows that the mistakes he makes are also all his own. There is no one else to blame. The child will have to pay a particular price for wrong decisions, and that price comes in the form of mistakes. But mistakes are good – the more he makes the faster and sooner he will learn.

Never reprimand a child for making mistakes, compliment him/her instead for his willingness to have a go and try something different. The mistakes are the price which you as a parent and he/she as a child have to pay for financial freedom.

The Business Brain Can you say you have a good business brain; one that can see business opportunities and work toward them? Can you see a good money-making opportunity when it stares you in the face? If you answered 'No' don't worry, neither do most other people.

Give your children a chance to answer 'Yes' by enabling them to learn about business as youngsters, when mistakes are far less costly. Give them the early experience to arm them with the knowledge and financial literacy they'll need as adults. I know this is only one of the many important strands in the upbringing of any child, but it is one which is often overlooked. Learning the fundamentals of money management is the first step in your child's financial education. Just think of the advantages to your grown child when he is running a small business if he has already mastered the essentials of collecting money, budgeting, investing and even sensible borrowing. Most businesses fail because their owners lack budgeting and planning skills. Don't let it happen to your child.

A Child's Business When I was in Form 1 (Year 7 in today's school system) I set up my own little business with the sale of football stickers. At that time, a radio station was promoting itself by handing out stickers for car bumper bars. I wrote to the station, pointing out that there were 30 children in my class and asking for the same number of stickers, covering all the different teams. When they arrived I sold them for 10 cents each, or three for 20 cents. As soon as one lot of stickers arrived I would send for another 30, always maintaining an adequate supply. I made good money back then on the sale of those stickers.

I realised, however, I was doing all of the work so I employed another student to help with selling, providing him with stickers for five cents each, which he then sold for the full retail price of 10 cents. I was paid in advance, so that he made money only if he actually sold all of his stickers which, when you think about it, was similar to working on commission, or you could see this exercise as him running his own little business. We both made good money, but I was making more money with less work. In other words, (of course I didn't know it at the time) I was leveraging my own time, or buying back some of my own time. In effect, I had sold a sticker selling franchise.

Just think what a learning experience that was. I came up with the idea and the means and now I had someone making money for himself and making money for me as well. This part of the money I was making came from passive income (earned without physical effort on my part). Other students asked if they could get on the bandwagon. I could have become greedy and agreed, but I considered the long-term effects, finally deciding that this would not have been a good move as it would have flooded the market with many sellers but there would be the same number of buyers. I reasoned that if I were to open up another franchise I should do it in a different school, so that one franchise would not affect the profitability of the other.

Others could have followed my lead if only they had known what to do. I certainly learned something about the law of supply and demand, not realising until much later that I could probably have charged more than 10 cents per sticker. In turn that would have exposed me to another lesson in life – that in every market, supply and demand sets a 'correct' price. Using my franchise operation as an example, a price rise would have forced me to closely observe the effect on my income, with a decline in overall profit telling me I'd done the wrong thing, and would have to learn to sell at the correct price for that particular market or find a different market. Anyone can sell anything at a cheap price but if the profit is not there then it is just a waste of time (and possibly money).

My own little sticker franchise introduced me to many

of the problems adults come across in running their own businesses. Even though it was a very small enterprise I was learning by playing the game.

Promote Your Child's Business Whatever you do, don't knock a child's ideas and aspirations for getting a start in business. Many parents extinguish burning desire in their children before they can even begin to experiment with their own great ideas. Encourage your child's entrepreneurial activities. Most parents would prefer to be able to boast to their friends that their child has become a doctor or holds down a senior post in a large corporation rather than, say, that their child has opened a pet shop business. Don't try to convince your children that they must work for an employer because it is 'safe and long term'. The truth is that those who see no alternative to working for someone else for the rest of their lives are victims of 'employee bondage'.

As parents, we owe it to our children to broaden their horizons by exposing them to the business world with its many avenues to a satisfying living as well as to the traditional, professional occupations. In doing so, we give our children true freedom of choice in determining their future directions.

When children start out in their own little businesses, the lessons learned from their many mistakes make their next business so much easier to tackle. The adult with experience of some childhood business has a great advantage over his less experienced peers when it comes down to the real game of business, because in the business world, those who have the most business experience win the game. Age has no bearing on business ability. Previous business experience has a huge influence.

Parental Example Make no mistake about it, your children watch what you are doing, even when it seems they are not paying enough attention to what you say.

That is why it is so important to set a good example in the area of money management, and why I strongly advocate that parents include their children in any discussions on the family budget. Rather than close it off as a subject not to be talked about at the dinner table or when the children are listening, discuss money openly with the whole family; after all they are likely to be affected by any decisions made.

When considering that possible move to a larger house (and how it could be financed), include the children in the discussion group. Or even some smaller purchase such as the new dress costing $200 but which you can't justify, since it will be worn only a few times. This creates opportunities for questions and explanation of the reasoning behind various decisions. Children want to know why you think the way you do, and before long they start playing the game of money management in their own minds. Your children should know that, say, 22 per cent of your income each week goes into an investment portfolio. Initiate a weekly allowance and show (and encourage) your child how to save a large percentage each week, spending only what is left over on things they like. But leave the choice to them.

Learning to Delay Gratification Whenever we invest money today to gain a financial benefit at a later date, we are practising delayed gratification, a concept not all that difficult to understand, but often tough to put into practice. On the other hand, when we give children money every time they ask for it we are practising instant gratification, undoubtedly the most destructive obstacle we can put in their way as they try to learn responsible money management. A freely available, continuous flow of money invites financial suicide.

In such an environment, the child can never learn to save and invest, and can't begin to understand that there is a time factor associated with saving money. What we spend today we will not have to spend tomorrow. The child must get that message and make an early start to planning the use of money on a longer timeframe than one or two days. The teenager who puts money aside every week will see the possibility of buying that first car without the need for borrowing. In my view, he/she must not borrow for his car and thus must save until he/she can afford to pay for it, experiencing at first hand the benefits of delayed gratification, a very powerful lesson that will make future decisions on delaying purchases so much easier.

When a child forgoes those small but desirable items such as food, audio disks, clothing or the latest fad, in favour of saving money for some much larger purchase such as a car, the concept of opportunity cost becomes much more easily understood. The child who ignores this lesson won't be in a position to buy without taking out a loan, a step I would never recommend. For me, buying a first car with loan money is not an option.

The Child's Bank Accounts Open bank accounts for your children as soon as they enter school, and – most importantly – make sure they become familiar with the detail of their own accounts and that they add to them on a regular and planned basis. It's also helpful in driving the lessons home to allow the children to organise their own money. You might consider giving them $10 each to spend in their own way. When you feel they are about to waste money on a purchase, don't hesitate to tactfully express your view – but don't prevent them buying if their minds remain made up. On the other hand, when the money runs out and another highly desired goodie appears, don't on any account hand over any more money. Let them get the message: the money's gone, and that's it. It's a lesson we all have to learn, along with the ability to budget, and while the learning curve can often be steep, rest assured they will learn that careful budgeting will leave them with money to spend.

Credit cards may seem evil to many people, and I agree that if they are used incorrectly, problems certainly can occur. But having said that, I believe all teenagers should have their own credit cards, even while they practise delayed gratification and save today for things they will need further down the track. Credit cards can be a useful tool in teaching and enforcing money discipline.

The teenager may have a $500 limit, but agrees to spend only what can be paid off completely by the end of the interest-free period, from monthly income. Interest must never be paid on this card. Furthermore, the money available to pay the card bill must not include the, say, 25 per cent of monthly income allocated for saving and investment, which remains the first priority. This is not always easy, but it provides a very practical lesson on the art of budgeting, calling for our teenager to work out, well in advance, the amount of money that must be available on the day of reckoning.

Precisely the reason why 80 per cent of the population get into bad debt situations at an early age, and then spend the rest of their lives trying to get out of it is because they haven't learned how to budget. Everyone must learn how to budget and the younger you start, the better. RULE 1: You can't spend more than you earn. And that means learning to live within your means. Financial independence is within reach for anybody who can live within their means and has understood that simple point from the time they had money to manage.

It is far easier to stay out of debt than it is to get out of debt, and it doesn't take many brains to work out that the further in debt we go the worse the situation becomes. Accordingly, never lend money to your children unless you can see that it is going to save them money later on, or make them money. Nor should you ever buy anything that will decrease in value with money you don't already have.

4

A 'GOOD, SECURE JOB'

A 'Good, Secure Job' has been the downfall of many people. The first experience of collecting a regular income came for many of us with our first real job. Do you remember yours, and did you enjoy it? Was it a good, secure job?

Let's face it, employees work for someone else at a fixed rate while that someone else (the boss) employs them to (hopefully) make him or her rich. Along the way, employees will often accept a low rate of pay in the knowledge that if they push for a higher rate they may no longer have a job. Job security, therefore, could go out the door should they mention a higher rate of pay to the boss. It must also be understood that the employer will pay the least possible to retain an employee, although the offer could be a little higher should there be a risk of losing a valued employee. Then again, it is often the case that the employer anticipates such a situation and already has another enthusiastic worker ready and willing to step into the breach and take over the workload anyway.

These days, employees must appreciate that their continued wages income from a particular job can no longer be guaranteed. It could disappear at any time; there is no longer any such thing as a safe job. Now that redundancy and closure of businesses are an everyday occurrence, it pays everyone, relying on a wage for their income, to be fully prepared. It is one more good reason to get your investments working for you very soon.

MY FIRST JOB

In my own case, apart from working for my father, it was not until I was about 15 that I got my first job, and my first wage. It came about as a result of helping my father at shearing time during the summer holidays, when he contracted experienced shearers. Travelling from farm to farm each season, the same group of shearers came to our place just about every year. As they ended their two-week spell on our farm one year and got ready for another farm the following day, I was asked if I would join them. I was ecstatic; this would be my first job away from the farm.

My father often advised me to get into the habit of always giving more than I got when it came to work and pay, pointing out that this approach would bring in as much work as I wanted. The shearers, who had seen me at work on the farm, knew full well that I was capable of hard work at that time. I have no hesitation in repeating the advice of my father: by being willing to go that extra step, and developing the habit of giving service and quality over and above your wage level, your reputation as a willing and valuable employee will be established.

With this sort of recognition, there is likely to be keen competition for your services no matter what your work, as well as prospects of higher pay and enhanced security. The contrasting attitude, 'I would do a better job if they paid me for it, but only a fool does something he isn't paid for', helps no one. Employees seldom receive a raise because they promise a better performance. The raise generally comes only when improved performance is demonstrated. Some people 'get by' doing as little work as possible, but that is all they get.

FIVE YEARS FROM NOW

Employees need to review progress in their jobs from time to time. To find out where you will be in five years time in your job, take a look at how far you have advanced during the past five years. If progress is slight, don't expect much movement in the next five years. This applies to your financial life as well.

Many people have said to me that they hope to begin investing and/or buying property and shares over the next few months. When they take a hard look at themselves and see how little they have invested over the previous five years, then you can guess that there is not likely to be much happening in the next five years. That is, unless they make some drastic changes. If there is no change in their actions then there will be no change in their results. And that applies to the jobs we do.

People who dislike their jobs immensely but still get out of bed every morning to go through the same routine should give the matter some serious thought. If they are hoping something will happen at work to suddenly make them love their work they might as well give the job away. It won't happen, and there is no reason why our jobs should make us miserable.

Why do people go on doing jobs they dread without looking out for something more suitable or more satisfying? It's a situation that makes life very scary, and should not be tolerated. Life is to enjoy, so find a way of experiencing life to the full – and that means finding a job you love and can excel in. Find something you love, and both satisfaction and money will usually follow automatically.

Of course, it is not possible to love every single aspect of our work, but if after working at a job for five years your dreams are not being fulfilled, then quit. Unless you change the pattern of the past five years, the results also are unlikely to be any better in the next five. People who, for whatever reason, remain in jobs they don't like, usually find that they are worse off in the long run. Sometimes it is debt which forces people to remain in particular jobs, but even then, the reality is that the situation often worsens. The noose is slowly tightening, choking them by degrees.

While I agree that some aspects of life won't be easy, and there will be periods in which the going can be tougher than others, it is possible to make life very easy, and very rewarding by working at it. Where is your job taking you? Have you aspirations to taking charge, or are you happy with what you are currently doing? If so, that's fine.

Many people say they don't make enough money at their jobs, but if they made more would they actually like their jobs any more? I wonder. There are people who go hopping from one job to the next in hope of eventually finding the ideal job which will make them happy, not to mention rich. Unfortunately, they often think the new job is great for the first year or two before boredom sets in again. Time to hop off to the next job.

I recall well my own decision to complete Year 12 studies, mainly because my father – who said I could return to the farm if I wanted – insisted that I had an alternative career, since the farm may not always be able to provide for two families. So I went to college to become a teacher, for no better reason than the nine weeks of holidays each year. As well, two other members of the family were teachers who seemed to have a good time. However, at 23 years of age, when I began to realise that I was spending everything I earned, it dawned on me that I would have to do something about it. But what?

The first was to focus on keeping money rather than spending – over the next two years I managed to save almost $19,000, and this from an income of about $17,000 a year. Remarkably, I was putting about 50 per cent of my income into savings.

The second step was to move into a small inexpensive flat where, living by myself, I had few temptations to spend (I had already found that I spent much more when I was out with friends). How did I force myself to do this? My pay cheque went into the bank as soon as I received it, to be withdrawn $100 at a time – but only when all my cash was spent and my wallet empty.

If the dollars ran out on Saturday, there was no money

to spend until the banks opened again on Monday. This was my own way of disciplining myself to save. It definitely worked.

Are you adequately paid in your job and have you felt for some time that your job offers you very little satisfaction? Is your heart still in your job or do you need something different? I know many people see their jobs as little more than a daily nightmare; they wonder how they will survive the week. So why don't they quit?

In many cases it is because there is too much debt, usually from personal loans which take such large lumps out of each pay packet. Do you work like a dog in the belief that it is hard work that makes people rich?

Many of us in paid employment are so busy doing our jobs that we haven't the time to stop and question how it is that someone else can make twice as much but still seem to have a lot more spare time. Few people give time to working out how they can become financially free, or contemplating why they have never made the financial grade. Worse still, there are many who have given up on the idea of financial freedom because they wrongly believe it is out of their reach.

THE TAX TRAP

The harder we work as employees, and the more we are paid, the higher is our overall income, but as our income rises, so too does the percentage of our income going out in tax. Employees are taxed on their gross income and then left with the rest to pay their various living expenses. I can tell you it's quite different in business.

Businesses are taxed in almost the opposite way; in business or where investments are concerned, the income is first used for expenses and tax is paid only on the remainder. Take the example of your private house. You receive a net weekly or monthly wage (gross wage – tax = net wage) and then you must meet such house-related expenses as repairs and payment of interest on your housing loan. This certainly is not the case when the same house is purchased as an investment property. You receive the weekly or monthly income (from rent with no tax taken out) and deduct first house-related expenses such as repairs and payment of interest on your housing loan. Then, finally, you will pay tax (or may even receive a tax refund) on the money left after expenses. This is a huge advantage which will be explained in greater detail in the chapters on property.

The point is that very few legal tax breaks are available to employees, in contrast to the excellent tax breaks available to the investor. When we earn an income in a typical job we are actively working for our money. When the income is from investments our money is doing the work for us. In business, people you employ are working to bring in money for you.

A word of warning. Not all businesses are like this, certainly not those set up by people keen to leave their careers as employees in the hope that they will no longer have to work. People like this have failed to do their homework. Typically, they buy a business just big enough for a few staff to run and it's not long before their profit and loss statements show that they can't afford not to be in the business themselves; the business doesn't earn enough money to support the extra staff needed to give the owners time off. These people have simply bought themselves a job – they don't own a business. The business owns them.

My idea of a good business is one which is a genuine investment capable of making money even if the owner is not physically working in it. As the owner of the business, I want complete freedom to choose whether I show up for work for 50 hours a week, 10 hours a week or perhaps not at all. In most cases working many hours in the business is a must for the owners during the first few years at least, but if there is no end in sight, then I argue they have done nothing more than buy themselves a permanent job, not really a business at all. To add insult to injury, this permanent 'job' will usually take many more hours of the owner's time than was the case as an employee.

AND IT GETS WORSE!

The biggest bills faced by most wage-earners usually involve the tax they pay, closely followed by interest on the mortgage for their own home. And, remember the money left to pay interest has already had the tax removed through the pay packet. Wage-earners generally believe they will become richer merely by increasing their income, but what higher earners actually find is that even though they may receive a $10,000 pay rise over the years, they lose close to 50 per cent of it in extra tax, because they have moved into the highest tax bracket. Their $10,000 windfall has shrunk to little more than $5000 in one hit, but that's not all.

Now that they have $5000 per year more in their pocket they are able to buy the bigger house or the newer car, which calls for that bigger loan they can now 'afford' to pay off. The loans (or, more correctly, their repayments) don't have to increase too much to chew up and swallow the entire $5000. Five thousand dollars amounts to $96 a week extra, but if the house mortgage is increased by only $60,000 at an interest rate of 8.5 per cent, their repayments ($60,000 × 8.5 per cent) would rise by $5100 – that's already $100 more than their pay rise after tax. Are they any further ahead?

When job-seekers go hunting for their next job the size of the pay packet is often their only criterion (I'm not saying that the pay packet is not important, but it certainly should not be the decision-maker). There are two far more important criteria. You must love the job, or you must see it as a stepping stone to the next advancement. When we love the job we're in, it is reflected in our performance and pay rises tend to come along automatically as our enthusiasm, growing skills and knowledge of the job are recognised by the smart boss as one of the reasons for his increased profits. If the rewards don't come look for another position, and don't hesitate to give notice when a better position is found. Let's face it, there can't be anything worse than having no money left at the end of the week and having to face up each Monday morning to a job we'd rather not be doing.

Don't be misled that your next pay rise will make you a great deal wealthier. The two don't always (or even often) go together. We all know many people on extremely good incomes but virtually broke, because they have no financial knowledge. The larger pay cheque doesn't solve their problems, and it won't solve yours. Instead, look at the pay cheque simply as the source of your initial cash flow. Your boss has done his job and paid you; now do your job and pay yourself by investing a firm percentage of your pay packet every payday, without fail. It is your job to make yourself rich, don't expect your boss to do it for you.

And the time to start is now – not five years down the track. Losing those five years will cost you a fortune in money and in time. Picking up a second casual job, or even a third, won't solve financial problems. The situation won't change for the better unless money habits change. Don't be scared of money, nor the lack of money. Learn to respect money and what it can do for you. Study it as you would your favourite football team or cookery book. Money has great power which can be made to work for you rather than against your interests.

We all tire of working long hours and doing extra jobs, and – as it becomes more and more scarce – our spare time begins to mean so much more to us. If this sounds like you, think about your money management. Money can help 'buy back' all of this lost time if you allow it. The important thing is to work with it, and not to waste it.

5

BAD DEBTS . . . BAD FUTURE

If you don't have money in the bank to buy that pushbike, TV or car, then don't get any of them at all. These days it is so easy to buy most things with credit cards, which is fine when the cash is available to pay off the card by the due date (and I mean pay it all off, not just the minimum requirement). Credit cards can be an asset, but they also pose some obvious dangers.

Young people can get into the habit from an early age of using various cards, including those issued by department stores, which typically have a spending limit of about $500. The dangers are obvious and the consequences often long-lasting. Incorrectly used, credit cards can plunge teenagers (and adults) into a debt roundabout, with a continual demand for debt repayments. Caught out, those on the roundabout pay off the minimum required and then find that next month their overall debt has grown again, thanks to an interest rate of at least 14 per cent on most cards.

It is not easy to get off the debt roundabout, which seems to (and does) travel faster and faster. The situation becomes even worse when they decide it is time to buy a car, despite being $1000 or more in debt and with no spare cash on hand. The only answer they know is to raise a personal loan through a bank or car dealership, again at a fairly high interest rate. Now, they are in a different ballgame, paying off a liability which is depreciating in value. As they reduce their loan commitment from, say, $10,000 down to $6000 over a few years, the value of their car also goes down, from $10,000 to $6000 at best – so they still have no equity in their asset.

Don't get me wrong. I'm not against borrowing. We need to borrow to invest. I regard borrowing to buy an asset as good borrowing. However, if we borrow to buy liabilities which decrease in value over time or even lose their value immediately, then we are into bad borrowing.

ASSETS AND LIABILITIES

In a later chapter I will look at how high our net value of assets will need to be if we are to enjoy a very comfortable lifestyle in our retirement years, but first let's look at what net assets are.

ASSETS are things you own which either bring in income or are growing in value. Houses, shares and cash in the bank are usually seen as assets even though they may not always be increasing in value. They can actually decrease in value sometimes but will usually increase in value over the longer term. These assets will make up the bulk of what I would invest in. A profit-making business is also an asset, and businesses that lose money are seen as liabilities.

LIABILITIES are those things that cost us money or are decreasing in value. These liabilities might include the car, the TV, the boat, the swimming pool or most of our house contents, although some are necessities we really can't do without. However, with many of our possessions, we wouldn't even know they were missing unless they were on a shelf in plain view all the time. Surely there is a message there. Go through your wardrobe and list all items of clothing you have worn only a few times, or – worse still – haven't worn at all. There will always be a few, and these are the very things we would not buy in the first place if our goal was to invest better.

NET ASSETS are the value of the assets minus whatever loans you may have. For instance, if your house is worth $150,000 but carries a loan of $120,000, then your net house asset ($150,000 – $120,000) will be $30,000. It is simple to work out total Net Assets. Just add the value of all assets together and then subtract the total of all loan obligations.

If becoming financially free in Australia is possible for nearly everyone, then why don't more people do it? The answer is that more people don't try because they think it is almost impossible; they have the wrong information in their heads and need to get the correct message. The key they require is called knowledge, and where finances are concerned, ignorance of that knowledge is certainly holding people back. Fortunately for those who want to do something about it, all they need is right there in front of them, just begging to be used. Walk into any bookstore and there will be a complete section on finance. Check out the financial newspapers, magazine and book titles and put your feet on the path to drastically improving your own position and becoming financially free.

As I pointed out earlier, financial independence won't occur quickly, but with the will and the right attitude, rest assured it will come. It's all a matter of commitment, experience, self-education and time. If you actually give it a go but have difficulty becoming financially free in the years ahead, look again at the rules that govern the building of wealth – and be honest with yourself: are you actually observing them?

BORROW ONLY TO INVEST

Good debt will make money for you but bad debt will send you backwards, financially speaking. Look at it this way; borrowings for assets are working for you, and borrowings for liabilities that lose value have you working for your borrowings – the bad debt has control of your life. When you don't have the money and therefore go without (perhaps a new pair of shoes) until funds are available, you are practising delayed gratification. If you haven't the money but must have the shoes so badly that you bring out your credit card, then you are getting into a very bad habit from day one by spending money you don't actually have.

We need to be very clear about this, and the few exceptions that may apply. We don't borrow for liabilities (if the purchase produces no income and/or will not increase in value then it is a liability). If the purchase will save money in the long run then it could make sense to use borrowed money if the cash is not available, for example, to borrow for the new suit which could help clinch that all-important job.

WHAT KINDS OF LOANS DO YOU HAVE?

People who can't save and have no investments usually have completely different kinds of loans from those people who do invest. The people I am referring to often have loans on most of their major furniture. Their credit card account is as full of clothes bills as their wardrobe is full of clothing, and their car is being paid off over the next five years at an interest rate much higher than any investment interest rate. Usually, they have the latest in sound equipment and hundreds of CDs, some of which they will never get around to hearing more than once, but they will keep on buying more and more anyway.

Then there is the behaviour of those with no spare money, when they are lucky enough to receive a pay rise. More often than not they reward themselves, buying an extra item a week. It doesn't occur to them to put this extra wage income, and a little bit of their own money, into an investment property that will appreciate in value, while the consumable item they buy as a reward will soon be worthless.

About 90 per cent of the population follow this sort of scenario. They should be able to work out that by following the crowd they will end up in the same state as the majority: broke.

You must pull away from the majority and do what the other 10 per cent do if you want to build wealth. Don't buy little things to be put away in the cupboard, never to be seen again. Cute at the time of purchase, they become mere extra mess cluttering up the cupboards after a few short weeks. Check out your wardrobe, your loans and your eating habits. Is most of your income going to investments or to your present lifestyle? It is possible to enjoy a great lifestyle now if you wish but it will be to the detriment of that lifestyle in the future. Don't borrow for consumable items. Borrow for appreciating assets only.

Bad debt is one reason why many people remain in jobs they don't enjoy but can't afford to leave because of its 'security'. They must keep the job because bills must be paid weekly; and the major bills are usually interest-related. Many teenagers now have credit cards before leaving school, and even at that early stage, need to have some continual and secure income. Therefore, at first, any job will have to do since they have debt repayments coming up on a continuous basis. They must have the money to pay their debts, and you will have heard them saying, 'I need that job'.

Getting out of debt has a lot to do with attitude. People talk about what they will do 'if' they get out of debt, but this is the wrong sort of thinking. They must discuss what they will do 'when' they get out of debt.

DON'T COMBINE YOUR DEBTS

No doubt you've heard of debt consolidation, that is, the combining of all your small debts (credit card, car loan and the loan which covered your TV set) and adding them to the house loan, which has a lower rate of interest. *DON'T DO IT!*

Think about it. If you have all these small loans then you obviously do not have the self-discipline to manage them and pay them out, nor the self-discipline to buy only when you have money available. You will find, just a few months after combining all of your loans, that you again take your credit card to the limit and buy that new item. Now the scenario is even worse than before, your debt roundabout is moving more quickly, and it is more difficult to get off. Whatever the form of your loan commitments, the larger your bad debt the more interest you have to pay, and all with after-tax dollars. The result is obvious – less money left from your pay packet to do other, more satisfying things. Your standard of living is in a word, declining.

Obviously, this is the opposite of what we want. We all want our standard of living to improve, but for that to happen, we must budget properly, and part of that is to promise ourselves that we will never borrow for unnecessary items.

WHICH LOAN SHOULD YOU PAY OUT FIRST?

We have debt, most of it is bad, and something has to be done. We have a furniture loan at 12 per cent interest, a credit card balance sitting on $4000 at about 15 per cent interest, a $10,000 car loan at the rate of 10 per cent, and the house is also mortgaged. Which do we pay out first?

The first thing we have to do without fail is *not buy one more thing with a credit card or incur any other debt until all those on our list are paid out.*

Then, as we have to continue meeting our home payments, just make the minimum monthly payments and no more on your home loan. Next, we clear our credit card debt, because it has the highest interest rate (15 per cent). The furniture loan (12 per cent) comes next, followed by the car (10 per cent).

Naturally, the quicker we pay off debts the better, since

remaining debt will decrease with each payment, bringing down the total interest payment required each month with it. Therefore, if we can keep up a set level of payments, the amount going to interest will be less because we are paying more off the principal. By paying the same amount every week a snowball effect sets in, with the debt shrinking with every payment. Incidentally, this snowball effect works in the opposite way when we accumulate assets; our investments increase in net value at an accelerating rate as we acquire more and more investments.

Directing every cent of spare cash toward debt repayment can help get rid of debt quite quickly, especially if you adopt a policy of using your regular pay packet in the following way – pay off your debts first, pay your essential living expenses next, and then, and only then, spend the remainder as you wish.

It's surprising but true, that by paying out a credit card debt on which the interest rate is 15 per cent, we actually save ourselves the equivalent of a 30 per cent return on the same amount of money invested in a bank – and you certainly won't get that sort of return from any bank. Let me explain. The interest on your credit card is not tax deductible, so you pay it with money from which tax has already been deducted. Assuming you are in the top tax bracket, you are taxed at almost 50 per cent, which means that getting rid of the credit card liability is the same as getting 30 per cent from the bank on the same amount of money.

Let's look at it another way. If you receive 30 per cent interest on your bank deposit and are in the 50 per cent tax bracket, then the tax man would take half, leaving you with only half of the money earned, or the equivalent of 15 per cent. And you are still in debt. No bank will pay us 30 per cent interest (even 5 per cent is not bad these days) so there can be no doubt about what is to be done, empty those deposit accounts and pay out your debt.

Don't keep savings in the bank for a rainy day? Remove your savings and pay out your personal debt immediately. If money is required for that rainy day, use a cash advance on your credit card, making sure that you then clear the credit card debt as soon as possible.

Always remember that money in the bank is likely to go backwards because of inflation and tax, so use it to eliminate your loans immediately.

If $2000 is required to fix the car, forcing you to use your credit card, go ahead and do it. You know that interest will be at 14 per cent or higher, and that is fine, because you will pay off your card over the next couple of months. Won't you?

Look back over the past 10 years and work out your average pay, perhaps $28,000 a year – or $280,000 over the 10 years.

This may not be the only income coming into your household when a partner's income is included. If the partner also earns $28,000 we would have twice $280,000, or $560,000, available over the 10-year period.

How much would be spent on bad debt and how much on investment debt? Or has it all simply gone and you don't know where? Unfortunately this is the position of the greater majority who admit, 'I am on a good wage but I just don't know where it goes.'

WHY HAVE BAD DEBT?

Why do people get into such bad debt? The answer is that, in most cases, they don't see where it is leading. They don't even consider the interest being charged, paying much closer attention to the repayments they will have to make each month. When they think they can manage the repayments, they're happy. They often buy things they don't really need because they believe they 'deserve' it or, since they 'went without' as children, they don't want their own children to 'suffer the same hardships'.

If you have bad debt then it's time to analyse yourself. Find out what makes you borrow for things you can do without. When you understand the consequences of bad debt borrowing, will you keep doing it? Have you the self-discipline to deal with it?

ARE ALL DEBTS THE SAME?

We need to understand that all debt is not the same. What will it cost you out of your own pocket to pay out a bad debt of $30,000? At an average interest rate of 10 per cent it amounts to $3000 in interest per year, taking $3000 straight out of your pay cheque.

Assume you have good debt, a $30,000 investment debt that for one will be at a lower interest rate of about 8 per cent. The interest on $30,000 at 8 per cent is $2400 – but because this is an investment debt you receive a tax deduction. Those in the top tax bracket get almost 50 per cent returned to them by reducing the tax they have to pay.

Our $30,000 investment loan cost us $2400, but because of the tax deduction, we pay $1200 less tax. Therefore, we are out of pocket only $1200.

Why would you want bad debt if good debt will cost only 40 per cent of the bad debt total? Actually, it even gets worse – the liabilities bought with bad debt are worth less and less with time, while the assets bought with good debt will be worth more and more over time.

You lose both ways with bad debt. With good debt, you win both ways.

6

HOW TO SAVE

I find it interesting to see how many people believe that success is a matter of getting lucky, as if success is something just waiting to be handed to them. If you are one of those people waiting for good luck to smile on you, then you will be waiting forever. To get lucky, you will have to go out and find your own luck; in fact, you must create your own good luck.

It's true that we can improve our luck by putting ourselves in a position to grasp those chances that life sometimes holds out to us, but generally speaking good luck won't come to us. Luck is far more likely to come our way if we open ourselves to all possibilities by having a positive attitude and acting decisively. From that point on, the enthusiasm of our response to the particular opportunity will almost always be the deciding factor between being lucky and being unlucky.

I don't consider my wife or myself lucky because, quite honestly, we earned it. Our success came from hard work, risk taking, and a burning desire to succeed. Our financial success is the result of a continuous process of learning from various individuals, learning from books, and – most importantly – learning from doing. Make no mistake about it. Nothing but knowledge and hard, continuous work, backed by good health, will ensure real and permanent success; there is simply no substitute. If you don't want to work hard, the goal of financial independence will elude you.

Part of the luck you make is learning where to save. People used to advise me to put 10 per cent of all wages into savings and investments, which I agree is very good in principle. But when you are young, what is to stop you from putting, say, 60 per cent of all wages into savings? Don't say that can't be done; plenty of people have set the example, and those who have succeeded would tell you that it is far easier to save if you can steer clear of the debt roundabout. Believe me, that makes saving – and so many other important things – so much harder.

Anyone aiming to achieve financial independence must come to grips with saving, and the sooner saving begins (and the higher the level), the sooner financial independence can be expected. Today, people who don't wake up to this fact until they are in their thirties come to the sad conclusion that they'll have to drop any ideas of retiring much earlier. But the good news, even for late starters, is that, yes, you still can.

A teenager who sought my advice had a familiar story – although he was employed on a reasonable wage for an 18-year-old, he found it was not possible to save. By the end of each week there was nothing left of his weekly income (he was on $18,000 a year). He had no car – he was fortunate enough to be able to walk to work each day – and lived in a one-bedroom flat costing him $70 a week. As well, he worked in a restaurant where he could get a good meal for just $2 on any night he was working. This young man could not identify where most of his money was spent – he had absolutely no idea. My advice? Completely change your spending habits. Invest first, then spend the rest.

He was told to begin paying into his investment account first, followed by the essential bills and only then, personal spending. In fact, his usual pattern was the other way round – spending money first on lifestyle choices, then bills and, finally, investing anything left over (in his case, nothing). However, he was motivated enough to agree to put the first $100 from his weekly pay packet into his investment account – and then to budget the rest. This meant recording in a small notebook, which he carried with him, every dollar of expenditure.

By the end of the second week, with $200 in his account, this young man expressed his amazement at how relatively easy the first two weeks had been, and furthermore, he was sufficiently encouraged to commit himself to this level of saving for the entire year. And he did, bringing his savings for the year to $5200 – a lot more than most adults will save even when living as a couple with two wages. What surprised him most of all was that he still had some money left over at the end of the week. This prompted him to put an extra $10 away every week, an amount he agreed to consider increasing even further if he again found this level of savings well within his means.

WRITE IT DOWN

The young man above found it easy because he had learned to budget and to diligently use his notebook to write down every item of expenditure. His priorities had changed, the number one aim now being to save the $100 from his pay each week. It's not uncommon for people to begin listing their spending, but the habit of writing it all down often lasts only a couple of weeks, if that. The benefits are obvious; by recording your spending it is easy to identify where the money is being wasted.

As an example, let's look at buying just two cappuccinos per day. That's a bill of about $150 a month on those drinks alone – and that translates to a yearly total of $1800. While on the subject of food, how about buying food while at work, perhaps as much as $10 a day. On that basis, your food is costing $2500 (cappuccinos not included) in a 50-week year, and that is just while you're at work.

Credit cards, with one proviso, can be a good method for keeping track of your spending. Use them for all purchases if possible, but on one strict condition – that you pay back your monthly bill completely by the due date. If you don't intend to do that, then don't use the card at all. (I cover credit cards in detail in Chapter 17.) One obvious drawback with credit cards as a record of spending is that it is not practicable to use them for many smaller items, which brings us back to the notebook for that all-important record of all items, great and small.

STAY AT HOME

Young people are usually very eager to leave home, to live by themselves or with friends. That is understandable, and certainly has a number of advantages. However, there is also a downside, including the fact that it becomes much more difficult to save, for rather obvious reasons. Saving is so much easier if young people live with their parents for as long as possible, often rent-free, and in many cases being charged only a fraction of the rents paid in the big wide world. Whether or not board is paid, eating with the family is another of the big at-home savings which makes it possible to place a large percentage of weekly income into an investment account. The weekly investment can be as high as 60 per cent of income, with the added bonus that those living at home may occasionally get the use of the family car.

PAY CASH FOR YOUR CAR

I know everyone wants to have their own car as soon as possible but giving in to that particular desire can be very costly, and can put you into debt for years. As for the overall cost of car ownership, just read the car magazines. You need to be aware that it is likely to cost you much more than $80 per week just to have your car in the garage, without adding in the cost of petrol and other running expenses. Any person interested in saving should postpone buying a car for as long as possible; it will certainly save them a lot of money (provided they don't spend their cash on other things they don't need).

It is possible to survive without a car. Try finding other means of getting to work, perhaps travelling with someone going in the same direction or workplace; even if you pay for their petrol you will still be far ahead. Using public transport as far as possible will also save a lot of money.

Of course, it won't always be possible to avoid car ownership, and at some point you will definitely need one. When that time comes, my strong advice is that you postpone buying a car until you can pay for it with cash. Try not to buy a car with borrowed money, even if it means ignoring the $25,000 beauty of your dreams and settling for the $10,000 two-owner sedan in the unwanted shade of orange. That will give you real motivation to save for the next car.

Many people will spend more money on their cars in a lifetime than on their homes, without giving real thought to the fact that their cars depreciate in value while their houses become more valuable. When you consider that the family car will be worth less and less every year while the home increases in value, year after year, you'll understand why the car has to be classed as a liability.

If you must get a car loan see if your parents can help you first before looking elsewhere. If they are able to help, they are likely to charge lower interest than will be available from banks or finance companies. Where a finance company will charge you around 10 per cent (hunt around for the best deal), your parents may be satisfied with around half that, perhaps 5–7 per cent or less. Of course, borrowing from parents imposes a responsibility to repay the loan (both principal and interest) as quickly as possible. From the point of view of the borrower, often a teenager experiencing his or her first real financial transaction, it is also desirable that parents insist on charging interest on this type of loan and that arrangements are made for a minimum monthly repayment. This can be an important learning experience for young people venturing into the world of debt, and they need to fully understand their obligations to make agreed payments by the due date. This is excellent education; learning by doing rather than relying on theory. Parents who don't charge interest for this type of loan 'to help their children get a good financial start' run the risk of actually hindering the youngster's financial education. It is all part of learning how to budget correctly, and management of a family loan – apart from more generous provisions – should be treated no differently from any other more formal loan arrangement.

UNWANTED LUGGAGE

I see a lot of money wasted on what I call unwanted luggage, those things we buy because we would like to have them, and not because we actually need them. It is, for instance, the new pair of shoes we bought to go alongside the two quite similar pairs in our cupboard (they looked so good in the shop that we just had to have them), or the new watch (the old one still in perfect condition). Computers are the go these days, and they sometimes come under the unwanted luggage heading, especially the replacement computer with all of the latest technical updates. The older model goes into the children's room so they can have their own. Even though the older computer still does everything we need, we nevertheless waste our money on the newer model.

Short-term thinking is at work when we buy these kinds of things. Often the decision to buy them is made because of the emotions aroused at the thought of owning them, followed all too often by the realisation that we had no real need for them at all. How often have you done this? I definitely have and probably not for the last time.

INVEST MORE THAN 10 PER CENT

If you decide to invest, why settle for 10 per cent – why not try for 20 per cent, 30 per cent or even more? Almost anyone can reserve 10 per cent of their gross income for investing, but few people actually do. As a matter of fact, most people don't invest at all.

I would urge everyone to get started by earmarking 10 per cent of your income for investment purposes, and when used to this idea, to increase contributions, perhaps by as little as 2 per cent per month. It would go something like this: in January, save or invest 10 per cent; in February increase this to 12 per cent; in March go for 14 per cent and so on throughout the year. With better understanding and diligent budgeting, this gradual increase is quite easy, the benefit shown clearly in Table 6.1 (I have assumed a weekly income of $500).

Putting money aside for investment may seem very difficult at first, but it becomes easier and easier as you stay with it. The sum of $160 per week may seem a lot to invest for some people, while it will look very easy to others. A young employee still living at home or a young couple putting one entire wage into investments will find the 32 per cent mark very easy.

Table 6.1: Invest more than 10 per cent

Month	Percentage	$ Income per week	$ Invested
January	10	500	50
February	12	500	60
March	14	500	70
April	16	500	80
May	18	500	90
June	20	500	100
July	22	500	110
August	24	500	120
September	26	500	130
October	28	500	140
November	30	500	150
December	32	500	160

It is very important that the first step with the weekly pay packet is to put the investment money into its own account, with payment of bills the next priority and the remainder available for any other purpose – perhaps to celebrate that small but important $100 first investment which puts your feet on the path to becoming a millionaire.

Don't forget: just one small step at a time will take you just about anywhere you want to go. It is not a question of how much money you make, but what you do with it that counts. Use your pay packet in the best way possible, and that means making your pay packet work for you.

FRIEND OR ENEMY?

A final word on the pay packet. It can be your friend or your enemy. Which it will be depends on how you choose to use it. How about using your pay packet to underwrite a large loan to buy that bigger house, more upmarket car or wardrobe of more expensive clothes? If that is your choice, you will be in effect giving these material things a measure of control over your life, perhaps for a very long time. It commits you to staying in that job simply to ensure you can pay your debts, a sad situation to be in, but one faced by the 80 per cent of the population sentenced to this jail, never to be released.

Are you in this jail, and has the key been thrown away?

7

INVESTMENT STRATEGIES

Most people see investing as placing money in a bank at a fixed interest rate. Nothing could be further from the truth; this is one of the lowest yielding investment strategies you could follow if you do it over a long time. The value of your money will be eroded by the effects of inflation and you will be missing out on far better returns available in other investment fields, such as shares and property.

A long-term investor must lean toward investments that return long-term growth. Those who prefer to leave their money in fixed interest accounts need to understand that the buying power of money in a bank is not protected. The $100 we spend today will buy far more goods now than the same $100 spent in a few years time, and for two simple reasons – the price of goods is always on the way up over the longer term, and the value of today's dollar will go down in step with inflation. So, if you leave your money in the bank for 10 years, it will certainly be safe, but its buying power will diminish dramatically. Inflation is the investor's best friend, and the saver's worst enemy.

We have to certainly begin saving before we can invest, but we don't want to leave money in a bank account too long. The interest we receive on bank deposits is taxed at a marginal tax rate; those on the 47 per cent tax rate lose almost half of their interest income to the taxman. And if our after tax return is less than inflation, then we are really going backwards.

Let me explain further. If we invest $10,000 at 5.5 per cent per annum we receive a return of $550. We then have to pay tax at, say, 30 per cent, which equals $165. This reduces our return to $385 ($550 – $165). Our account now stands at $10,385.

During the same period, the prices of goods rise by the inflation rate of 2.5 per cent, which in effect means that those things we could buy for $10,000 at the beginning of the year cost $10,250 by the end of the year. Now we see the true level of the increase in our wealth, which is down to $135 ($10,385 – $10,250).

We can now work out that our true or real return on our $10,000 term deposit investment is a mere 1.35 per cent – ($135/$10,000 × 100/1 = 1.35%).

As you can see, money left in the bank has very little investment power. You must invest in growth assets, assets that increase in value such as property and shares. They have the added advantage that rent and dividends also increase over time, along with tax advantages. The tax effective approach is to invest to receive little income over and above your wage or salary by concentrating on receiving capital growth and by accumulating assets.

Buying your own home, which does not add to your

current taxable income but does offer the potential to grow in value, is an ideal investment. It is then a very good investment strategy to pay off your own home as quickly as possible, since the interest on your loan is not tax deductible. The interest repayment is made from after-tax dollars and not before-tax dollars, as is the case for an investment home. The Australian situation is different from that in some overseas countries, such as the USA, where the interest on a private home mortgage is fully tax deductible, reducing the urgency to quickly pay out a mortgage.

I don't necessarily think you should aim to pay out your entire personal home loan straight away. Instead, after paying off part of the loan, borrow against the equity that you now have in the home and use it as a deposit on your next investment. When you redraw this money for investment purposes the interest you pay on the new borrowings is tax deductible. Even though your private home stands as security for the money you redraw to invest, the interest on this loan becomes tax deductible because the purpose of the loan is the purchase of an investment. The purpose of the loan determines whether the interest is tax deductible or not. The type of security being held by the bank is not relevant.

HOW DO WE INVEST?

How do we make money work for us? First of all, we must have some, and that means we have to find a way to generate some savings. How you do this will depend on what 'good' money habits you are willing to keep. As soon as you have enough money for a deposit on a house, buy one priced on the cheaper side of the average price of houses.

Buy in an area you find desirable and in which you could live comfortably – never buy in an area in which the average person would not want to live. These areas hardly ever appreciate in value. Remember, we are looking for investments that will appreciate well in value but won't necessarily bring in a high income, which would add to your taxable income. A large percentage of this extra income would be lost to tax.

Pay off some of the loan on your first house as quickly as possible. When extra equity available reaches about $20,000, borrow that amount to provide the deposit for your next house. Borrow as much as you can for the second house, fixing the interest rate for as long as possible. Bank loans will be discussed in detail in the later chapters, including which loans you should use.

Any extra income from now on should go toward paying off your first house until again you have enough equity to raise the deposit for a third property. Again, raise the largest possible loan on the third house. As before, extra income goes to pay off the first home, and as your equity puts you in a position to borrow again, say, about $10,000, use this sum as well as borrowing another $10,000 to buy shares. When borrowing for shares, never exceed a loan/value ratio of 50 per cent, that is, if you have a partial loan on shares, never borrow more than 50 per cent.

Assume for a moment that you have shares worth $20,000. To leverage these shares my advice would be to restrict loans to a maximum of $10,000, giving us a loan/value ratio of 50 per cent = $10,000/$20,000. If you borrowed $15,000 and used $5000 of your own money to make up the $20,000 your loan/value ratio would be 75 per cent.

I would regard this as far too risky, and I don't know of any institution that would lend you money on a 75 per cent loan/value ratio when it comes to shares. The usual limit is 70 per cent, but by borrowing more than 50 per cent you create unwanted risk, and – as a very conservative investor – I never take any unnecessary risks. As an investor, control and minimise risks as much as possible.

COMPOUNDING

For something that can make such a huge difference to investment returns over time, compounding is really quite simple, as the following examples show. Let's assume you buy shares paying out a dividend of 5 per cent per year, and that in addition to the dividend, the value of the shares increases in value at a rate of 10 per cent a year, giving us a total return on our investment for the year of 15 per cent (10% capital growth + 5% dividend). Two further assumptions are that the total return (capital growth + dividend) amounts to 15 per cent each and every year, and that the dividend – rather than being withdrawn and spent – is put back into the investment under a dividend reinvestment plan, a common practice with many shares. Now you have, say, $1000 worth of shares and your investment increases by 15 per cent every year.

After one year, your initial investment has grown to $1150, that is, $1000 plus 15 per cent (which is $150). A simple way to work out the increase and to establish the new level of your investment is to multiply the $1000 by

1.15, which gives you that $1150 total. Carry out a similar calculation at the end of the second year, multiplying $1150 by 1.15, and you have a new total of $1322.50, boosting your asset by $172.50.

You can now see that as well as an increase in total value, the actual amount by which the investment increases each year is also on the way up, as Table 7.1 demonstrates.

Table 7.1: Compounding at 15% over 10 years

Year	$ Start	$ Increase	$ Total
1	1000	150	1150
2	1150	173	1323
3	1323	198	1521
4	1521	228	1749
5	1749	262	2011
6	2011	302	2313
7	2313	347	2660
8	2660	399	3059
9	3059	459	3518
10	3518	528	4046

Look carefully at Table 7.1, and note that in the first year the increase was $150, while in the tenth year the increase was $528 – and remember, you have put no more money into the shares at all yourself. Your total investment after the 10 years has gone from $1000 to $4046, an increase of just over 400 per cent. To determine what our $4046 will be worth after another 10 years, simply multiply by four (the new total will be $16,184). After a further 10 years (a total of 30) our initial $1000 will have grown to $64,736 ($16,184 × 4).

When considering Table 7.2, take an even more careful look at what happens to our investment total in the fourth 10-year period.

Table 7.2: Compounding at 15% over 40 years

Year	$ Start	$ Total
00	1,000	4,046
10	4,046	16,184
20	16,184	64,736
30	64,736	258,944
40	258,944	

So, 40 years after putting in our $1000 we will have $258,944 – and that does not include any extra money we would invest during the period. Imagine, if we began with $4000, our investment asset would exceed $1,000,000 within the 40 years.

Let's look at saving $300 a month. Invested at 10 per cent and left to accumulate, it would be worth about $1,100,000 within 35 years, but, of course, to be able to put $300 away every month we will need to set up a budget.

I wonder how many people get to the day before payday to find there is virtually no money left; and wonder why it is so hard to build up a bank balance. One thing is for certain, it won't happen by accident – budgeting is essential, and the earlier you begin and the earlier you begin investing, the easier by far it is to achieve financial freedom. When you invest your money it begins earning a return. If you reinvest the returns the original investment begins compounding, that is, earning a return on its return in addition to the money you make on the original investment. It may sound like stating the obvious, but the longer your money has to grow, the more it can grow. When you are young and starting work at the age of, say, 20, your invested money has far more working years ahead of it than if you begin investing at the age of 45.

In Table 7.1, I gave the example of compounding over 10 years, turning the sum of $1000 into $4046, which in turn becomes $258,944 over 40 years, as shown in Table 7.2. Remember that our assumption was for your money to compound at 15 per cent per annum. In this book I will show you how to get 30 per cent, 50 per cent or even better returns on some of your overall investments. To demonstrate the effect of improved returns on the long-term outcome, let's say you received 30 per cent on your $1000 investment. You might think that because you are receiving 30 per cent now compared with the 15 per cent of the original example, you would end up after 10 years with twice as much money. That seems reasonable: 30 per cent return is twice the value of 15 per cent, so on that basis, instead of finishing with $4046 in 10 years, you will have twice that amount, $8092. Let me amaze you by demonstrating just how wrong this $8092 calculation is, but don't just take my word for it; get out your calculator and work out for yourself the total amount available from your $1000 invested at 30 per cent for 10 years, compounding.

The simplest way to do this is to multiply $1000 by 1.3 for the first year and then multiply the total for each following year by 1.3, until reaching the 10th and final year. I've started the calculations in Table 7.3, but I leave it to you to carry out the remaining calculations so that you really get the idea.

Table 7.3: Compounding at 30% over 10 years

YEAR	$ START	$ INCREASE	$ TOTAL
1	1000	300	1300
2	1300	390	1690
3	1690	507	2197
4			
5			
6			
7			
8			
9			
10			

Your $1000 investment should now be worth about $13,785 (don't worry if you are a little bit out). But do make sure you fully understand what you have just done, and if in doubt, please go back and read over the last few pages again. It is important not to get lost here.

By growing from $1000 to $13,785, your investment is worth almost 14 times as much when invested with a 30 per cent return, a far cry from the four times growth in your investment when the return was 15 per cent. And if you think that is exciting, take a look at where your $1000 investment will be in 40 years if invested at 30 per cent. Just multiply $1000 by 14 for every 10-year time span, as I've done in Table 7.4.

Table 7.4: Compounding at 30% over 40 years

Year	$ Start	Times	$ Total
00	1,000	14	14,000
10	14,000	14	196,000
20	196,000	14	2,744,000
30	2,744,000	14	38,416,000
40	38,416,000		

Look again at the difference:

$1000 invested at 15 per cent for 40 years = $258,944.

$1000 invested at 30 per cent for 40 years = $38,416,000.

That is a phenomenal difference of about $38,159,056 over the 40 years. Think about it.

Let's look again at compounding, but in a different way. This time we'll invest $10,000 in one go and see how it grows during 40 years at 20 per cent return. I'll give you the answer – over 40 years our $10,000 compounds to just about $15,000,000. If you think that I am labouring the point – that you should be compounding your money for as long as possible – then you would be right, and I don't apologise for it. It is extremely important that you fully understand this concept. Play with it on your calculator until you are satisfied that the sums do add up. Seeing is believing, and I assure you these numbers don't lie, but they do tell a story.

This is why profit and loss or asset and liabilities statements mean more to me than the owner's description of how good their business is, or a person's boasting about their ability to save and invest. Give me the numbers every time.

As a school student it was drummed into me that reading and writing were far more important subjects than mathematics, and I was convinced for years that this was in fact the case. However, because my English, comprehension and reading levels were poor throughout my student days, my inclination took me in another direction. Since I was good at figures, I always chose classes that included maths, a judgment that has certainly paid off in my adult years. But don't imagine for a moment that you need the maths of a rocket scientist to understand and manage personal finances and investing. The beauty of it all is that the mathematics required is very basic and all sums can be done on a $15 calculator. I'll prove it. With this basic maths I'll break $1,000,000 down into smaller segments, and let the numbers tell the story.

Firstly, can you get your hands on $1953 within a year's time? If you can, you have done all you need to do in the first year on your road to becoming a millionaire. Secondly, by the end of your second year toward becoming a millionaire, can you have saved $3906? If you can, then let me break down for you what you have just achieved.

By the end of year one you have net assets worth $1953. By the end of year two you have net assets worth $3906. You have just increased your net assets by 100 per cent, and in our example you haven't even begun to invest the money or begun leveraging your time.

Now let's assume that by the end of the third year you have saved a total of $7812 – again increasing your net worth by 100 per cent. In Table 7.5, I'll show you what would happen if you increased your net worth by 100 per cent per year for each of the next 10 years.

Table 7.5: Doubling net worth each year

Year	$ Net Assets
1	1,953
2	3,906
3	7,812
4	15,624
5	31,248
6	62,496
7	124,992
8	249,984
9	499,968
10	999,936 + $64 = $1,000,000

Again, we are just playing with numbers and it might look too simple, and I hear you say it is not possible to keep doubling your net worth. Don't forget that it was possible to double your net worth in the first year (not too hard either) and again in the second year, and it should therefore be possible to keep on doing that – after all, you now have more assets at your command.

Throughout the targeted 10 years, you would be placing some of your income into investments each year. The more invested the better off (and by far) you will be, and the earlier you begin investing this larger pool of money the better, with dramatic effect on the final net worth figure.

So, how can you begin to increase your income and boost your investments, giving you that all-important start on the road to financial independence?

- You can buy investment property and borrow against it to buy more.
- You can get a higher income job.
- You can buy shares and leverage or borrow against them to buy more shares.
- You can become self employed and begin leveraging your time and money by employing staff.
- You can buy a business returning a very good income and work to further increase its profits.

None of this will fall into your lap. Nothing can be achieved without the will to succeed and hard work, but I assure you it is possible. The first step toward investing is to get a deposit together somehow, and this is the barrier which most people hit when they first come to an understanding that they need to get involved in investing. And again, the answer is deceptively simple – learn to save.

CAPITAL GROWTH

We can expect that over the years our assets will increase in value at, say, 9 per cent per year as a result of capital growth, that is, increase in value of the asset itself. As our assets go up in value so does our equity, and we can borrow more money against that equity with a view to buying more assets, again borrowing as much as possible on each of these new assets. Remember, if the purchase we are thinking about won't produce an income or grow in value then it is not an asset, so don't borrow for it. We don't borrow to buy a car or a sound system. They are liabilities, not assets.

Table 7.6 summarises the point we've reached with the various investments already discussed in this chapter.

Table 7.6

	$ OWN MONEY	$ BORROWINGS	$ VALUE
House 1	30,000	100,000	130,000
House 2	20,000	100,000	120,000
House 3	20,000	100,000	120,000
Shares	10,000	10,000	20,000
TOTAL	80,000	310,000	390,000

What happens if prices on each of the investments rise at 9 per cent per year for the next five years, and for this example we don't even take into account gains already made since buying our first house.

Take a close look at Table 7.7.

Even when we remove the loan amount of $310,000 we are left with $290,064 in net assets ($600,064 – $310,000). So, the $80,000 from our own pocket has grown in only five years to $290,064. This is an increase of $210,064

($290,064 – $80,000) or, to look at it another way, our original $80,000 has increased by 263 per cent in that period.

Table 7.7

	$ Total Investment	% Rate of Increase	$ Year-End Total
Year 1	390,000	+9	425,100
Year 2	425,100	+9	463,359
Year 3	463,359	+9	505,061
Year 4	505,061	+9	550,517
Year 5	550,517	+9	600,064

With assets now worth $600,064 we can borrow about 80 per cent, or $480,051 ($600,064 × 80 per cent). After allowing for the $310,000 already borrowed, that means we can now borrow an additional $170,051 for further investment ($480,051 – $310,000). This allows us to buy another three houses, each with a deposit of $56,684, using the new houses themselves as security for the loans. Or, sticking with my advice never to leverage more than 50 per cent on the purchase of shares, we could buy $340,102 worth of shares ($170,051 × 2).

However, assume that we do buy the next three houses at $150,000 each, and track them along with our other assets over the next five years (with the same growth assumptions) in Table 7.8.

	Assets after 5 Years	600,064
	Three New Houses	+450,000
	Total Gross Assets	**$1,050,064**

Table 7.8

	$ TOTAL INVESTMENT	% RATE OF INCREASE	$ YEAR-END TOTAL
Year 1	1,050,064	+9	1,144,570
Year 2	1,144,570	+9	1,247,581
Year 3	1,247,581	+9	1,359,863
Year 4	1,359,863	+9	1,482,251
YEAR 5	**1,482,251**	+9	**1,615,654**

Take a look at the difference in growth levels from the fourth to the fifth year; total assets have gone from $1,482,251 to $1,615,654, an increase of $133,403 in only one year. This level of increase – what I call passive income – will occur each year. Also, the rents we receive from houses and the dividends obtained from shares will be on the increase. Depreciation allowances for buildings, fixtures and fittings all provide tax deductions, positives which mean that each house costs very little 'out of pocket' each year, and soon creates a positive cash flow.

I am painting a very general picture here, and it's true that there will be other positives in the process as well as some negatives we haven't yet taken into consideration. But if you now have a general understanding of the direction in which we're heading you are well on your way.

In general, from your *income* buy as many *assets* as possible. With the *income* from the *assets* and your own *income*, buy more *assets*. As the *assets* grow, use the extra *equity* in these *assets* to buy more *assets* and keep on using the *income* from your active *income* and from the growing *assets* to buy more *assets*. The key words required to become financially free are: Income, Assets and Equity.

Another Scenario Let me assume you are living in a house which you partly own, and that in today's market, it is worth $200,000 but with an outstanding home loan of $90,000. You know that, since it is your private home, interest on the $90,000 loan is not tax deductible and that the interest payments come from your wage on which tax has already been paid. You might not yet be comfortable with buying other investments, so your first goal is to pay out your own home loan as soon as possible. As a result, you budget very tightly, determined to pay off the home loan as quickly as possible. When the loan is cleared, which might have taken you and your partner another three years, the house could have increased in value to about $250,000.

You are now in a position to take out an Asset Builder overdraft account, using your home as equity. It doesn't mean you must use all of the money available in the account, and you pay interest only on the amount you actually use. Since interest is calculated daily, and only on the actual balance, it is an advantage to pay off the overdraft as soon as money becomes available. On a house worth $250,000 the bank is likely to lend up to 80 per cent of valuation, that is, $200,000 ($250,000 × 80%). With this $200,000, you could put down $50,000 deposits on three different houses each worth $200,000. The remaining $50,000 would enable you to buy $100,000 worth of shares, provided you were willing to borrow the second $50,000, using the shares themselves as security.

What assets do you now have?

Own Home	250,000
House 1	200,000
House 2	200,000
House 3	200,000
Shares	100,000
TOTAL	**$950,000**

On this portfolio you would expect to receive about a 9 per cent return in capital growth over the long term. Table 7.9 shows the situation you'd be in after five years, without adding any more assets or investing any more of your income.

Table 7.9

	$ TOTAL INVESTMENT	% RATE OF INCREASE	$ YEAR-END TOTAL
Year 1	950,000	+9	1,036,000
Year 2	1,036,000	+9	1,129,000
Year 3	1,126,000	+9	1,230,000
Year 4	1,230,000	+9	1,341,000
YEAR 5	1,341,000	+9	1,462,000

Note that in year five your assets increased by $121,000 in passive income, all on the initial asset of your private home, worth $250,000. The return on your initial asset value at that stage stands at 48 per cent for the year ($121,000 ÷ $250,000) and growing. Without increasing your investments but instead paying off some of the loans, your minimum passive income would be $121,000 a year. Not bad for five years of investing without adding in any additional income you may have from earnings or rental income increases. And, of course, you could also be borrowing more money against extra equity to buy more properties, if you wished.

We now know that in five years your gross assets grew to $1,462,000 and your loans total $700,000, leaving net assets of $762,000 ($1,462,000 – $700,000). Your net assets have grown from $250,000 to $762,000. The $512,000 you made in that period represents a return on the initial $250,000 of 205 per cent ($512,000 ÷ $250,000). Remember, we are talking about five years of investing, not just the one year.

INVESTING IN SHARES

How can you multiply your money by buying shares? In 1991, I bought shares for about $5.50 each. Today they are worth about $26.00. Assume that you bought $100,000 worth of these shares, using only $50,000 of your own money and borrowing the other $50,000, with the shares themselves as security. The $100,000 invested in 1991 has now increased to $473,000. So, take away the $50,000 of borrowings and you have turned your own $50,000 into $423,000 in nine years. (By the way, the interest on the

$50,000 loan would have been covered by the dividend returns from your full $100,000 shareholding.)

The increase from $50,000 to $423,000 represents an increase of 746 per cent over nine years, about an 83 per cent annual return on the original $50,000; and that works out on average for the nine years at $41,444 per year. This is a very good return where you put in only $50,000 of your own money. Having built up to $423,000 worth of net value shares you could borrow up to $423,000 and buy more shares, doubling your portfolio to $846,000 – all started with only $50,000 of your own money.

My point here is that you must invest in growth investments rather than park your money in interest bearing accounts, unless you know you intend to invest it somewhere in a relatively short time. Why would you leave it in a bank at about 5 per cent a year when – as the last example shows – it could be growing by as much as 83 per cent average a year, a difference of 78 per cent.

Everyone is Different. I know we don't all think the same, and you will in any case be the one who determines the amount you will invest and how aggressively. Of course, there will be many unable to borrow to the extent shown in my examples, and that's fine; you have to find your own comfort circle and invest only to the extent with which you are comfortable.

In investing, knowing yourself is extremely important. It is essential that the particular investments you choose suit your personality and lifestyle. If you can't sleep at night because you are worried about them, then maybe they're the wrong investments for you. It could be that you need to do a bit more homework, and work out more carefully where the unwanted risk lies. If you still feel uneasy it may be better either to sell the investment or lower the risk level by reducing the loan commitment.

TAKE LESS RISK

Those keen to take less risk might look at the following scenario. Assume you own a house worth $200,000, and a $90,000 loan. Over the next three years you pay out the loan and, due to inflation, the house is now worth $250,000. You decide to buy only one investment house and use $40,000 from equity in your own home to get a deposit and borrow the other $160,000, using the new purchased house as security over this $160,000. You now have $450,000 worth of houses and your total loan is $200,000. As you receive any income, use it to reduce your loan, decreasing any risk involved (although I don't see any risk at all). After all, if you buy in the right area, at a discount to the price of building a house on that same block, there is no risk, and the purchase of the house will bring you a profit.

In our 'less risk' scenario, we now have two houses, total assets worth $450,000 – so where does that leave us in 10 years? Well, I've started a table (7.10) and I'd like you to work it through to the 10th year (if you get your sums right you should come up with $1,065,000).

You still have a $200,000 loan, but even if you decided not to pay off any of it, your net assets would be $865,000 ($1,065,000 – $200,000). Turning an initial asset of a $250,000 house into $865,000 is a very good result for someone investing very conservatively. As you become more comfortable with investing, you may choose to look at other possibilities, whether in real estate or shares. It is entirely up to you.

Table 7.10

	$ TOTAL INVESTMENT	% RATE OF INCREASE	$ YEAR-END TOTAL
Year 1	450,000	+9	491,000
Year 2	491,000	+9	535,000
Year 3			
Year 4			
Year 5			
Year 6			
Year 7			
Year 8			
Year 9			
Year 10			

IS IT INVESTING OR GAMBLING?

If your investment strategies include buying land in Queensland because you've heard that the price will double in the next two years, then you are gambling and not investing. Millions of dollars have been lost in various investments, such as ostriches, emus and in futures trading, because the investors concerned have not done their homework. It is exciting to enter a new investment field, but as a newcomer to the game, you have so much more to learn than the experienced investor dealing in, say, futures trading over many years. I can't say how I would invest in the areas mentioned because I am not sufficiently familiar with them to even hint at what I would do. All I can say is that any investor should be extremely careful, and willing to do plenty of homework. While there are ways of making money in these fields, it seems clear that only a small percentage, perhaps 10 per cent, actually make money while the remaining 90 per cent either lose money or do well to come out square.

Don't look for a quick way to make your fortune overnight; it won't happen. If you want to gamble, try the horses and bet with your $100, but don't gamble on an investment you know nothing about. It could cost you thousands of dollars in a very short time. Aim to be a long-term investor and not just a 'flash in the pan' investor, and the longer the term the better. Develop a well thought out investment plan, and keep it clear in your mind, even though you will make changes as you travel along your journey to financial freedom.

Get started with a small investment if you wish, but the main thing is to at least start. Your serious learning won't truly begin until you put your own money on the line, whether you make or lose money. Believe me when I say your lesson will be more concrete if you lose money. Small investing will lead to big investing, if only you give it a chance – the longer you put it off the harder it will become; the younger you begin the easier it is. One of the greatest contributors to success in investing is time, so don't waste it.

It should now be obvious to you that the amount you save and invest today will determine your current and future standards of living. You may have to do without what you want today so that you can have as much as you want, and more, tomorrow. The opposite is also true. The more you spend today the less you will save and invest and the smaller your assets or investments will be in 10 years' time.

PART 2

Property – How To Invest Wisely

8

THE BRICKS AND MORTAR STORY

I know many of you reading this book will be saying that I make it all sound too easy. That's why I want to give an account of how we made our first investment when we bought our first home. I sincerely hope that by the end of it you will say to yourself: 'If they can do it, so can I.'

A friend of ours advised us, not long after we got married, to buy a house rather than rent. He said that that would leave us far better off in the long run. It took a while to convince me, and it was only after I learned more about his family that I began listening to every word of advice with great interest.

It turns out that his family had begun with very little, but had worked to build up many businesses over a span of 15 years and had become extremely wealthy. Fortunately for me, they became my mentors, persuading me later to go into business for myself, which Mary and I did two years later.

At the time, there was no shortage of advice; various

friends suggested all sorts of different ways of making the right decision. But whose advice should I follow?

I looked at what many of these friends had achieved. Although all of their advice was well intended, few of them had much or any experience in buying and selling houses of their own. From where were they getting their opinions? Why did some think one way and others the opposite? Again, to whom should I listen?

Our mentor family had bought and sold property particularly well. They had a track record of success in business and in investments, which made it clear to me that I should look to them for guidance, and no one else. Had my other 'advisers' had similar experience and successful records with property and finances, I would have carefully considered what they had to say as well. To my mind, it made so much more sense to go with people who had 'been there and done that'.

So now my advice is to listen to those people who can show they've been successful, and ignore those who 'know everything' about property and shares but don't actually own any themselves. These are not the advisers you want. Find someone who has done what you want to do or who now has the lifestyle you would like for yourself. Talk to them, and you'll find in most cases that they're very happy to help others who share the same hopes and dreams as themselves. It will pay you to find out as much as you can about these people; if they've written a book, get hold of it, or if they are involved in seminars, go along and listen to them as often as you can. Take every opportunity to work out how these people think.

Once our minds were made up, Mary and I spent all of our spare time over a couple of weeks looking at every available house. In 1983, the price for a 'good' house in a 'nice' area ranged from about $40,000–$80,000, with anything beyond that too big and too expensive for us. Since we were going to be in it for at least two years, and possibly three, we agreed our house would need to be a nice home, although we understood that it would not necessarily measure up to our ideal, long-term home. We had to buy knowing that we would sell in a few years.

The question of which kind of house would sell well within three years had to be considered, as well as carefully sorting out how much to pay and the best area in which to live. We found about five houses which suited our requirements, but still did not make a decision until fully comparing each and making up a list of all the positives and negatives we could think of. In other words, we did our homework – and we did it well.

We eventually selected and put in an offer on one house, offering only $1000 lower than the asking price of $45,000. The offer was immediately accepted. As it happened, settlement did not take place for some months because of some problems with the positioning of the house on the block. Our solicitor made sure that all problems were solved before settlement went ahead. In hindsight, we could have done a little more homework, which would have revealed that the vendors owned a block of land and were ready to start building. In that case, they probably needed the money and may have accepted less than our offer of $44,000, perhaps as low as $41,000. Offering

$41,000 would not have been a problem for us; had they rejected that first offer we could always have increased it. However, when they accepted our first offer we had nowhere to go, which may have cost us $3000.

But that was a useful lesson, and I have now learned never to offer the vendor's asking price. The vendor, assuming that the purchaser will bargain to some extent, usually adds something to the price to cover this, with most expecting to come down about 10 per cent of their asking price.

DO PEOPLE LOSE MONEY IN PROPERTY?

You will have heard of people who have lost money in property, but they will usually be first homebuyers or first-time investors who have not done their homework diligently. You must be in control of your purchase price and you must control your sale price – buy property where you know capital gains will be present at a good rate.

If you find that you have bought the wrong property in the wrong area then it is clear you did not do enough homework. Listen to real estate agents, but be aware that you will need to do your own homework. When you realise that the investment property is going nowhere, sell it for the best price you can get and accept the loss as a good lesson. Get on with your next move, do your research and try again.

If you have bought property but prices don't seem to have increased over the last three years, don't rush out to sell because you think you may have bought in the wrong area. Do your homework again. House prices can mark time. This happened in the early 1990s, when prices did not rise on a continual basis. Interest rates were very high at that time and there were many sellers; little demand but a lot of supply. In times such as this hang onto your property as the up cycle will most likely return, as we have seen since 1997.

If you are going to buy a property but still have no idea what the approximate market value is then *you have not done your homework*. You need to get out and research more properties. Often you will be sure you know the approximate market value of a property but upon inspecting a few more you might see that their selling prices are well below the property you are looking at, even though the houses seem very similar. You will then realise that the price on the house you are looking at is too high. The more you know about all properties in the same area the better and more educated is your guess at the true price of the property you are considering.

WHAT IS THE BEST PROPERTY TO BUY?

In many of the books I read and many of the seminars I have attended, writers and speakers suggest buying land within 12 kilometres of the business centre of capital cities. This is where, they say, you can expect the greatest capital growth. I don't disagree with this statement at all but up until today I have done very well without buying any properties in any capital cities. This doesn't mean I am not looking at city properties; I am actually researching properties in the middle of Melbourne at the moment. But I have always thought that I knew more about the properties in my own backyard, which is in the country, and I have bought all of my properties in the same country town, a market I have studied with great diligence. I know what areas to buy in this town and where not to buy. I know where the land value is worth more, for instance, because it is a very easy walk to the town centre. I have done my own homework in my own area.

I think it is important to buy in an area you know very well, rather than guessing about the best spots and trying to establish reasonable market values for areas you are not familiar with. The time spent travelling around different suburbs could be used better for more detailed study of houses in your own market, enabling you to pick up better buys.

Always look for properties that will be sought after by the greatest number, and then look for houses which you know you can buy for a price below market value. To do that, you need to know why people are selling; whether they are in a hurry to sell or whether they are just sitting on a house at an inflated price, not really pushing the sale along. Never buy a house which you believe is offered above its true market value. Always buy at a discount to market value. The only way to know what that true value is, is to study every house sold in an area over the previous three to six months and to look at every house currently up for sale. You will soon get a feel for the actual value of each house. It soon becomes possible to compare and identify the houses which are overvalued and those which come in at a discount. Go to every auction for any house close to the range of value you are looking for, and study these auctions well. Attend auctions even though you have no intention of buying, so that you can get a 'feel for the market'.

Don't hesitate to ask to go back through the house many times. You are making a very big decision, so make it very carefully. Make sure you inspect the property in all types of weather. If your first inspection of the property was on a fine day go back and have a look at it again as soon as you get a good downpour. There may be holes in the spouting you don't see until after heavy rain. The backyard might also be in a low-lying area, creating a dam outside the back door when it rains.

Check the neighbourhood at night. Has the neighbour parked his big semi-trailer truck at the front of his house, ready to start it up at four o'clock every morning? It isn't the sort of alarm clock you or your tenants will want.

If I was buying my first house today, I would look for the cheapest house I could buy, but let me make it clear; this does not mean that I would look for it in an area in which no one wants to live. The problem with many young families is that they do the opposite. They want to own a more luxurious house from day one, but because they have only enough money for a very small deposit, they are forced to take out a mortgage which is out of all proportion to their income. All their money goes to their mortgage.

You select an area in which 70 per cent of the population would be quite happy to live and then look for the cheapest house available, in which you would be willing to live for five or six years. Let me give you a quick example of this:

Say the mean price range of homes which would suit most people in one particular town is from about $80,000 to about $160,000. Other houses worth as little as $50,000 are available, but you would ignore these since they would be in areas where there would be little capital gain. The first step would be to carefully study houses in the lower bracket of the $80,000–$160,000 range, perhaps about $90,000. Look for reasons why the owners are selling. It is often the case that you will find a mortgagee sale, which is where a bank has taken over the house because the owners are not meeting their repayments. Often, banks will accept a lot less than the actual value. They simply want to get their money back.

I can't emphasise enough how important it is to study the market in which you are. Impulse-buying should never be a factor in the purchase of property. Study the market well and you will make the best choice when it comes to which property to buy.

It is very important to buy wisely. Obviously, the less you need to borrow, for your own home, the better. The higher the borrowing required to purchase your own house, the less attractive the investment. Therefore paying off some of the loan quickly also makes it a more attractive investment.

When we invest in our own homes, we use income on which we have already paid tax; in other words, we are investing after-tax income. And the cost of loans to individual (as distinct from investor) homebuyers is higher because interest payments on these loans are not tax deductible. This means that the higher your tax rate, the greater the saving to be made from paying off your house mortgage. If the interest rate on your home is 8 per cent, then paying off your home loan at a faster rate than the minimum requirement is the same as investing this extra money elsewhere for a return of 16 per cent.

BUY AND KEEP

Many people find it hard to comprehend why you would buy property and keep it even longer when they could have sold it for a good profit. They ask themselves the question 'What if house prices go down again?', as they have in the past and certainly will again in the future.

The reason why we keep the property is because over the long term of 10 or more years the property market has ALWAYS increased – and will keep on doing so. If you try to get in and out when you think property prices are low and then property is at a high price, you are becoming a short-term trader rather than a long-term investor. Traders can still make good money by doing this but they must read the market very well. They have to know or 'guess' the best time to buy and the best time to sell. If they are wrong they are likely to lose money on short-term ownerships. Traders frequently getting in and out also have higher costs for real estate agents, solicitors, and loan arrangements.

Investment in property is completely different from other forms of investing, and should always be regarded as long term. It doesn't matter if you buy at the high of the market because you know that over the long term your property will increase in value.

LEVERAGING YOUR MONEY

Investment property is one of the best ways of leveraging your money. If you had a $100,000 house and used only $10,000 of your own money and borrowed the rest, you can use the $100,000 home and some other equity as security for the loan on this property. If the property value increases by 9 per cent per annum on average, you would make $9000 capital gain in the first year ($100,000 × 9%), increasing your net worth by $9000 on an initial investment of $10,000. What return have you made on your money? It works out at 90 per cent ($9000 ÷ $10,000 × 100) on the initial $10,000 – a very exciting return when some people find investing in property lacks the excitement of buying the technical stocks in the stock market.

But if you are buying all of these investment properties and then using any extra income or equity in these properties to buy more properties, when will you start to see the income and when can you spend it?

As your portfolio begins to grow year by year you reach the stage at which your net worth increases by perhaps as much as $150,000 a year, all this even after you have used money for personal living as well. You might then decide not to invest in more properties or shares but instead to let the extra income pay out your lending on the shares. Your interest expenses will therefore decrease, allowing your overall income to increase. If this continues, the stage will arrive when you can't spend all of the income on yourself and you may as well put it back into other investments. You now have the choice.

As the years go by rent income also increases, again

providing more income. Nor should we forget share dividends also increase year after year, making more money available for spending or reinvestment into shares or property. So don't sell your properties and shares, but reduce the expenses in interest repayments instead to automatically increase your income.

9

INVESTMENT PROPERTIES

Before getting into the investment scene, it always pays to put your foot in the water and get a feel for the market. When Mary and I first bought property as an investment we had done very little homework, and I was not aware of many of the issues mentioned in this book. I had not been looking around at every house that was for sale in our country town. I had not studied the prices of other houses sold in the area during the previous six months. I knew that we had to invest in property but that was about all I did know. Since I had done next to no reading on how to choose a house or a desirable area, I wasn't even sure what price I wanted to pay for the house.

One afternoon I found myself at an auction looking through a house, about half an hour before bidding was to take place. The advertising board showed that it was a mortgagee auction. The real estate agent announced that ' . . . this house will sell at whatever price the bidding reaches'. (The seller usually decides on a reserve price below which they will not sell.) My understanding was that because there was no reserve price on this house, it would be sold even though the final offer may be well below market value. The terms of sale called for a payment of 10 per cent of the sale price on signing of the contract, with the balance on settlement in 60 days. These are common conditions for the sale of houses at auction.

I really did not know what to think of the house except that it needed to be tidied up. As the bidding began, I noted that there were only three bidders, a low demand which made me think the house would sell fairly cheaply. Bidding began at $38,000. I entered the bidding and before I knew it, I was the successful bidder at $44,000. By the time bidding ended my back was wet with sweat even though it was a cool day. I had been drawn into the excitement and determined to be the winner. I don't know how high I would have gone; perhaps I would just have kept going. This was dangerous territory.

I had to pay the 10 per cent deposit of $4400 immediately and I remember driving home to get the cheque book since I had no idea at the beginning of the day that I would have bought our first investment house that afternoon. The following day I had a meeting with the bank manager. He gave us another loan immediately in the knowledge that we had paid out our other loans quickly and would therefore be no risk for his bank. I asked for a principal and interest loan, setting a term of only 10 years. With principal and interest loans, minimum monthly repayments are required, but any amount can be paid into the loan account to clear the debt more quickly. There is no penalty for early repayment. However, to be able to pay extra off the loan, it is not possible to fix the interest rate, so a rise in the interest rate would cost more. Some banks now allow you to fix the interest rate and pay extra off the loan if you wish. In our case, interest rates were sitting on about 14 per cent, and I decided that instead of putting extra money into paying off the loan I would instead save money to raise deposits for more property investments.

Over the next few years we bought another two houses and two shop freeholds, that is to say, we bought the actual buildings and not the businesses in them, which continued as our tenants, paying rent for the use of the buildings.

Meanwhile, the tenants in our first investment house decided to move out after about 12 months. After some repairs and a paint job, this house was looking good and required no other maintenance work at all. The real estate agent said we could sell it for about $65,000. We couldn't believe that the price of a $44,000 house could rise so much in just 12 months, with only about $2200 on maintenance during that time. We were looking at a profit of about $20,000.

Our thinking at the time was that this was excellent 'income', and we put it up for sale. It was sold within a fortnight. At the time this seemed like such easy money. But we could have done even better. Because the property was now valued at about $66,000 we should have had the bank revalue it and with the extra equity raise a very good deposit on another house. Let's walk through what the possibilities were:

Initial price of house	$44,000
Loan	$31,000
Revalued house	$66,000
Possible loan	$46,000
Extra loan available	**$15,000**
	($46,000 – $31,000)

That $15,000 could have been used for a deposit on the next house. I would pay about $50,000 to $70,000 at the most for the next house, which meant that the $15,000 would provide a 30 per cent deposit on a house bought for $50,000, or – if the house cost me $70,000 – the $15,000 would give me a 21 per cent deposit.

There are many ways in which to maximise your opportunities by using investment properties to your best advantage. There are also many hidden traps you will need to avoid. In this chapter we will be looking at the highs and lows of investing in property.

BUYING TO INVEST FIRST

If your first home purchase is an investment house rather than one you live in, then you already have an asset on which tenants are helping to pay interest and other expenses, as well as helping you pay it off. Earlier I said you should not pay off an investment property, but – since this is your first property – this case is different. You do not own your own home yet, and you should pay this property off to the extent that you are comfortable with buying another investment property. If you don't plan to buy your next property for a year or more, then I would aim to pay off as much of the loan as possible. This gives you a great goal to help with your budgeting habits.

If over the next two years you pay out as much of the loan as possible, which might be up to $10,000 a year, you would have about $20,000 available, as well as a positive cash flow from tenants helping you pay off the loan. In this way, there could be about $24,000 of reborrowings available after two years. In addition, the house could have capital growth of about $16,000, giving you $40,000 to use for the next property purchase.

If you intend moving into your next property then, as your personal home, any loan interest payments will not be tax deductible. So if you can see yourself buying your own private home in the next 12 months you should stop paying off any more of your investment house. Instead, you should save it in an account for your new home, since you want the loan on this new home to be as small as possible.

Don't forget that your personal home is going to be at the cheaper end of the scale. Your main aim is to put most of your money into investment and to put very little into non-deductible personal items which in this case applies to your own home. Don't buy an expensive first personal home until you have many investments. Under this scenario, you soon have both an investment home working for you and your own home. From now on meet only the *minimum* monthly repayments on your investment home and change the loan to an interest-only, fixed interest rate loan. There will be a cost in changing the loan over but it will be well worth it; you now pay interest only on this loan. From now on, any extra money you have goes toward paying off your private home loan as quickly as possible. You will also find that there will be excess rent from the investment house, which should also be used to help pay out your personal home loan. Don't forget that your expenses such as interest on your own personal home are not tax deductible so you want to reduce this loan as quickly as possible.

Once you feel comfortable that you have reduced your personal loan enough, you can reborrow this money and use it for investment in your next property or into shares. You will have to do your own calculations and work out when you are comfortable to buy more investments.

In another scenario, you could move into your first home and rent out the second one. In this case, instead of saving for a deposit for your personal home and then moving into it, you would be far better off to move into your first investment house and make this your own home. By doing this you would not worry about putting savings aside for a deposit but you would instead pay off your first investment house loan. When you then move into this investment house as a private home, it no longer attracts tax deductible advantages, so you would keep on paying it off as quickly as possible.

When making arrangements for your next investment property, obtain the largest loan possible for your new investment. Fix the interest rate for as long as possible and make it an interest-only loan. Then you would not have to pay any principal off the new property loan, which attracts tax deductions, but would put every bit of available money into paying off your own home. Again, when comfortable that you have paid off enough of your personal home loan, you could reborrow against the equity in that home for a deposit on your third investment. Of course, you might be more comfortable paying out your own private home completely. Do what you feel more comfortable about doing.

Our Second Investment House One house Mary and I bought for $66,000 was from a mortgagee auction. We had been doing our homework for about three months and knew every house on the market, and believed we knew what they were worth. I knew how much we were willing to pay for them. I had calculated the value of this particular house at about $85,000. It had been left in a mess and needed some love and care – but not much.

We had just come back from the house and walked into the real estate agency. The agent asked us what we had just seen and his comments were: 'I have just seen the bank which has taken over the house. Offer them $64,000 and I think they'll be glad to take it'. I looked at Mary wondering whether we were talking about the same house, which I had valued at about $85,000. We immediately put in an unconditional offer of $64,000. Within half an hour we had negotiated $66,000. Within the next two weeks we turned this dirty house into a spotless, well presented home. We did most of the work ourselves and employed a professional cleaner for only one day. The total cost to turn this house around was about $400, plus our own labour. It has been rented ever since, and I could easily sell the house in today's market for about $145,000, but I have no intention of selling.

BUYING A UNIT

When considering buying a unit, look for a block of land with only two or three units on it. This is far better than buying a unit in a larger group of say, six, because most people living in units don't want to be surrounded by too much activity. Mary and I bought a block of land and built two units. The block could have accommodated three units, but they would have been smaller and not as appealing in the short term for tenants, or later on for possible buyers if and when we chose to sell them. If you live in a unit sharing a block with only one other unit, you are only likely to face disturbance from one other tenant; you know there won't be a party in each of the different units in a multi-unit property, night after night.

Mary designed the units and worked with the builders. I had no interest in this and she really enjoyed doing it. I was in charge of organising finance, working with the banks while she worked with the builders. Our units were fairly big and we spent more than the average to fit them out, providing us with two big units which were a little bit more up-market by comparison with other units in the town. We therefore could expect to attract tenants looking for something above the average and willing to pay above-average rent.

If you offer very homely homes with the few extras that tenants appreciate, such as en suites and large bedrooms, make sure that you ask enough rent for your properties. Find out what other landlords are receiving for properties of much the same standard. Don't undercharge; it is difficult to increase rent once a tenant has moved in. Charge the right amount for the property and service you are offering.

VACANT LAND OR HOUSE

Don't buy a vacant house block as an investment unless you plan to build on it immediately. If you think your block of land is going to be a good investment, think again. Let's look at the numbers because 'the numbers tell the story'.

You're going to buy a $40,000 block of land but you don't plan on building on it for, say, three years. You have $10,000 in the bank for a deposit. The interest rate for a loan to buy the block will be 9 per cent, while the interest rate on a personal home loan would be 8.5 per cent. At the moment, you're renting the house you live in for $160 a week. Taking all of this into account, what is it actually costing you to buy a block of land?

Rent $160 per week × 52	$8320
Interest on $30,000 loan × 9%	$2700
Total Annual Cost	**$11,020**

What if we were to buy a house to live in.

$150,000 house – $10,000 deposit	
$140,000 loan	
$140,000 × 8.5%	$11,900
Rent	0
Total Annual Cost	**$11,900**

How much more will it cost you to have your own home? $11,900 – $11,020 = $880 a year or $17 per week. You will only have to find another $17 per week to own your own home in comparison to buying a block of land.

What about capital gain (assuming value increases at a rate of 9 per cent annually)?

$40,000 × 9% $3600

$150,000 × 9% $13,500

Difference $9900 in favour of owning your own home.

You must also consider that your rent could move above the current $160 per week, leaving not much doubt that, as an investment decision, you are far better off buying a house than a block of land.

If you buy a block of land as an investment to sell in a few years time, the interest payment on the loan is not tax deductible. The block of land would have to be producing an income for you to claim expenses such as rates and interest as tax deductions. Therefore, if you have a block of land which you thought of as a good investment, you might be better off to sell it; using the tied-up money for an investment house will be a far better proposition.

MANAGEMENT OF INVESTMENT PROPERTIES

Have you heard the comment, 'you get nothing but trouble from tenants'? We have hardly ever had trouble with tenants, nor have we lost any money due to any tenant. Treat your tenants well and they will treat your house well.

All of my properties are managed by a real estate agent. She is excellent and knows what I expect – and I know what she expects from me as a landlord. The agent collects rent and approaches the tenant if any payments are late. Rent is automatically deposited into my accounts. There is usually a fee of about 7 per cent for this service but as you obtain more properties it is possible to negotiate a lower commission.

Rent is paid monthly in advance, in addition to which tenants pay a four-week bond, which means they have to find about two months rent before they even have the key to move in. If the tenant doesn't have the money, don't allow them in the house in the first place. Make sure you have good references of all tenants before you accept them. Don't rely entirely on a written reference, ring the referees and ask them some searching questions. This is one advantage in dealing through an agent.

The tenants applying for your houses have often rented through the agent previously and are well known. Make sure the agent tells you all about possible tenants before making any offers – you may know something about the applying tenant which causes you concern. In this way, you can help the agent. If your tenant requests the agent for some repairs, make sure that it is done promptly. The tenant will remember such positives and be happier about staying in your house.

Your agents are the experts in this field. Find a good one and stay with them. Give your agent the go-ahead to make their own decisions when requests come in from tenants; they know who will do the job quickly, who will do it well and who will charge a reasonable fee.

Have your properties checked yearly by someone who can see problems or foresee problems likely to occur if action isn't taken immediately. I employ a man to visit each property annually and clean out gutters, check trees or shrubs likely to cause structural damage and to report to me on all properties about any repairs or required maintenance. It could be something as small as rewiring the clothesline or rehanging a gate, or it could be a more major task such as painting facia boards or renewing rusted spouting.

Together we decide on the best course of action and he ensures that everything is done. I am not interested in doing small maintenance myself, since I could not be described as a handyman; I have other things I want to do with my time. If you can't do the job properly yourself, then employ someone who can.

BITING OFF MORE THAN YOU CAN CHEW

If you find yourself on the debt roundabout and it is now getting so fast that you can never see yourself getting off it then you might have to make some drastic changes. Your ego will now be your worst enemy. Consider selling the expensive house (worth, say, $250,000) and maybe the car (worth $35,000) to get yourself completely out of debt. Let's assume you have the following loan commitments:

	$ VALUE	$ LOAN
House	250,000	180,000
Car	35,000	20,000
Credit card	10,000 limit	8,000 balance
Second car	15,000	0
TOTAL	310,000	208,000

Your average interest on all of these loans would be about 9 per cent, so that annual interest would cost $18,720 (9% × $208,000). Remember that this payment is with after-tax dollars, since all of these items are personal and not investment items. You therefore sell the house and the car to pay out all of the loans.

$250,000 house + $35,000 car = $285,000 total.

$285,000 total − $208,000 debt = $77,000 cash left over.

You now buy a smaller house to the value of $140,000, which requires you to take out a $63,000 loan from the bank ($140,000 house − $77,000 cash available). However, against an asset worth $140,000, the bank will lend you up to $112,000 (80% of the property value, $140,000 × 80%). Since you need only $63,000 for this house you can use the rest for the next investment home. This means that with your $112,000 loan, you have $49,000 deposit available for an investment property ($112,000 loan = $63,000 house loan + $49,000 deposit).

You then buy an investment home worth $140,000 which will provide a capital gain of about $12,600 a year. With rent coming in on the new house plus the depreciation allowance and the cost of interest, you will find that the house will cost you about $600 a year out of pocket after including a tax refund. I will show you these calculations in Chapter 11. Interest on your $63,000 personal home loan will be about $5040 ($63,000 × 8%) which is not tax deductible. Rent coming in from the new house will be $9360 ($180 a week × 52 weeks). Interest payments on the investment house will be $11,200 ($140,000 × 8%).

In this example I am assuming that you are on the top marginal tax bracket. As well, all maintenance expenses on the investment house are tax deductible, an advantage not available on the private home.

Given that loan interest payments on your private home amounts to $5040 and the cash flow on the investment house is minus $600, the total annual cost to you of the two properties is $5040 + $600 = $5640. What is the difference in cash flow now that we have downsized our house?

Before, it was $18,720, but now it amounts to only $5640. That's a difference of $13,080 ($18,720 – $5640), leaving you with the $13,080 a year extra which can now be used for further investment. If you now go on to build up your investment portfolio over the next 10 years you can buy any house you want, or any car you want. And you need never go to work again if that's the way you want it to be. Are you willing to do all this?

Only you know the answer, but remember – if you give up some of the things you have now, then down the road you can have everything you want.

Is a Holiday Home a Good Investment? Nearly everyone would like to live down by the beach where they can walk along the sand each day and watch children playing happily in the water. It's easy to see how the emotional side of our brain can take over. However, in comparison with other investment properties, holiday houses down by the sea are not usually good investments.

The intention is always to use it every fortnight and during school holidays, which is fine for the first year, but by the time the second year comes around the holiday house is being used once a month or every second holiday. Most of the time it remains empty, with no rent at all coming in but many expenses going out.

Assume the house cost $140,000 and you obtained a loan for $100,000 at 8 per cent fixed interest on an interest-only loan for five years. It would cost $8000 per year ($100,000 × 8%). Rates and insurance and a bit of maintenance each year cost another $2500 a year, bringing the total out of pocket cost to $10,500 a year, or more than $200 a week.

If, instead, you bought an investment property elsewhere you would find that you could rent it out for about $140 a week, an income of $7280 per year. So let's assume that interest costs are the same at $8000 a year and that rates and insurance costs are again $2500 – we now have $10,500 in costs, income of $7280 and have a tax deduction of $3220. But, because you are bringing in income from the investment property, you can also claim depreciation for fixtures and fittings and for the building. Depreciation is discussed in more detail in Chapter 11. By owning a holiday home rather than a comparable investment property, you would be out of pocket by approximately $9000 extra per annum.

Perhaps you thought of letting out the holiday house for part of the year. Again, if letting it out on a casual basis so that it was tenanted for a minimum of one week but a maximum of perhaps three weeks at a time, the house would be empty more often than it would be full. Your rent might be good while the house is occupied, but this could be for as little as 12 weeks of the year. You then have to pay someone to clean it and it needs to be fully furnished with beds, refrigerator, washing machine etc, and your maintenance bills could treble.

If you think you need to invest for your holidays, buy an investment home which you know will provide good capital gains as well as good long-term rental income. With these investment returns, you can now holiday wherever you choose. Buying a holiday house at a coastal resort costs you money, and ties you to the same place for most of your holidays. Do you want to go to the same place year after year, or holiday after holiday?

10

HOW TO BUY PROPERTY

I have seen many people who have attended only one auction, and who end up buying a house for an inflated price. They 'love' the house, and they bid for it just as if they were in fact 'in love', with no rationality at all, but complete emotion. These people have not worked out what they consider to be a reasonable price and so have no price in mind at all. If they feel good about it then they will keep bidding.

This sort of emotion can make it hard for these people. They often go too far into debt, well beyond the repayments they will be able to make. By failing to do their homework, they risk putting themselves on a debt roundabout which may already be going too fast. Their emotion has put them in this position. The emotional centre of their brain has taken over from the rational part. Because this emotion is so much stronger than their rational thoughts, common sense goes straight out the window.

People often don't think logically when it comes to money. The real estate agent points out how lovely it will be sitting in the courtyard of your new house, next to the pool and watching the children laughing and having so much fun. You will have a great book in one hand and a drink in the other. Logic is no longer a consideration, emotion has 100 per cent control.

Don't buy a house because you become emotionally attached to it. The numbers must add up. If it is too dear compared to market value or you can't afford repayments then let the numbers tell you the story. Look at the figures. What will this one purchase cost you in terms of standard of living further down the track?

At auctions, listen to what other buyers want to find out about the houses, questions you might not have thought to ask. Never be scared to ask a question even if you think it is a silly question. I believe that *'he who asks the most questions will win the game'*, and for a very obvious reason – *'he who asks the most questions will then know more of the answers'*.

DEALING WITH REAL ESTATE AGENTS

You are in the business of buying a house for as little as possible. The more you can get for your dollar the better. Assume you find two houses, each with an asking price of $95,000, either of which you would be very happy to buy. Why not offer $85,000 for each house, dropping in a typed offer for each at the same time and informing the real estate agent that you have also put in an offer for another house. The agent will inform the vendor of the offer; make it clear that you have also put in another offer, and would then tell the vendor that the first offer accepted will be the house you will buy. The agent will push this point because he has a serious buyer with a typed offer, and he doesn't want to lose the sale.

This will then play on the vendor's mind. He'll be thinking, 'I have a buyer at this price, and if I don't accept, and quickly, then the offer might be gone for good. I may not get another offer for months. What should I do? I can't afford the repayments (or I'm shifting to another state) so I really should consider the offer seriously.' If you don't hear back from the agent in the next two days, phone and inform him that the offer remains unchanged. This makes the agent think and he might go back to the vendor with the advice that you are not willing to budge on price. The vendor knows where he stands. If one of the offers is accepted, be polite and inform the other agent that you have a sale and are withdrawing your offer with him. Now the agent knows the rules of your game, and knows that you are serious.

You will be dealing with these same agents many times with your future property investments, and if they know how you are willing to play the game, then they will work harder next time on the initial offer. So you now have a house for $85,000 on which you could probably receive a sworn valuation for $95,000. There is no need yet, since this is your private home, but if you were using the money for investment purposes, then you would have the house valued and obtain the highest possible loan. With stamp duty and buying expenses, your new home will have cost about $90,000. You will be able to raise a loan up to 80 per cent of the purchase price from a bank, totalling $68,000 in this case.

Always put an offer to an agent and sit on it for a while. Don't listen when the agent says there are another three very interested buyers. Perhaps there are, but how close are they to making a decision? Do they have to sell their own properties before they can buy the place you're looking at? Of course the agent wants you to think that if you don't buy now, you'll definitely miss out.

When making an offer, try to ensure it is not conditional on finance, which tells the vendor that finance will not be a problem; it is as if you are able to pay cash for the property. Organise your finance well in advance. You almost certainly won't have the entire purchase price available, but can scrape up the 10 per cent deposit required. With that as a starting point, build up as much money as you can save, beg and put together in a short time over the few months to settlement day. The bank will usually make up the shortfall to 80 per cent of valuation, and it is possible to borrow up to 90 per cent of valuation if you pay mortgage insurance as well. However, if you can get by without paying mortgage insurance then by all means do it. This insurance is quite expensive since it is calculated on the total sum of the loan, and not just the amount between the bank's 80 per cent and 90 per cent. In that case, the last 10 per cent of finance can work out very expensively indeed.

Finance was not a problem for Mary and me. For reasons outlined earlier, I saved like mad in the two years before we were married, putting aside $19,000, while Mary had $20,000 by the time house settlement was due.

As her $20,000 contribution shows, Mary is a good saver, achieving such a good bank balance even though she had been overseas twice, and had just returned from 12 months abroad. Anybody who has been overseas can appreciate how carefully she had to budget to survive financially over such a long period.

If you ever decide to sell a house for whatever reason, make sure you give it to every real estate agent in the area. If you go with a sole agency, you give this one agent exclusive rights to sell your house. Other agents therefore don't have your house on their books. The sole agency might push the sale of your house more because you have given it to them alone, but how many prospective buyers do you miss out on?

Look at the shopping centre you travel to most of the time, which is not far away from the house you are selling. How many real estate agents service the area – perhaps as many as five? Consider your potential buyers. If they are looking to buy a house, how many agency doors do they walk through to inquire about houses for sale? If they have travelled from a different location on a Saturday they might have time only to visit two real estate agents rather than all five. If your house is not on the books at either of these two agencies you could well miss out on a buyer even being aware that you have a house for sale. By placing your house with all agencies the buyer is likely to be told about your house at every agency, that is, the most possible times.

Some people buying a house are more relaxed using only one agent even though this could be to their own disadvantage. If a potential buyer goes into only one agency because their friend works there or for some other reason, they could again miss your home simply because you haven't placed it with all agents. Increase your chances of sale. Put that house with every agent.

It is also important that each agent has a set of keys to the house, garage and shed. Most people looking to purchase want to see inside the shed and garage as well as inside the house.

Type out a detailed list of everything the house offers. Agents sometimes won't even recognise some of the positives, and may not list them unless you put the details in front of them in writing. Get your camera and take a full roll of film of the house from every vantage point; pick out the best and present these to each real estate agent in proper photo folders, along with your detailed typed house description. The agents will probably want photos of their own, but don't forget that some agents may be lazy or haven't the time to get things done. Make their job as easy as possible so that your house is never disadvantaged as is the case when they haven't done their own homework properly. Sell yourself to the agent in the same way as you would sell yourself at a job interview. Don't undersell your house.

When it comes to price, ask initially for what you believe is the top price you could get. If there are no interested buyers within the first month the price tag can always be lowered. Give yourself plenty of time to sell. There are almost always buyers out there willing to pay your asking price. You just have to wait for them to come along.

HOW DO YOU BUY PROPERTY?

When buying an investment property make the settlement time as long as possible; don't ask for a 60-day or 90-day settlement, better still, go for 120-day settlement. Why is the longer settlement such an advantage? Let's say you buy a house on 21 March with settlement on 21 July, which is 120 days after your offer has been accepted. You have now given yourself more time to work with the banks and find the best available loan, and during that four months the price of the house may also have increased in a rising market so you may be able to get a larger loan.

When you seek a loan larger than 80 per cent of the purchase price you will need a sworn valuation on the property, and the bank will base its decision on this valuation rather than the purchase price. The bank usually relies on the purchase price as the value of the asset when it works out how much it is willing to lend you. The more you can get from the bank the better because then you can use any extra money to buy other investments.

The 120-day arrangement also gives you a lot of time to work out what sort of rent you should charge on the property, which hopefully will begin coming in from the day of settlement. You can afford to try for a higher rent because you still have a few months in which to attract a tenant. If no tenant has put up a hand for the property by the last few weeks before settlement, then lower the rent to a more average price to ensure the property is rented out from day one. Your letting agent will be able to help you here.

If the property becomes vacant before the settlement date, approach the vendor for access. Use the time to fix up the back fence, repair the blinds or even take care of those rooms which need painting. However, before doing this, check with your solicitor to make sure everything is fine with the progress of the sale. You might even be able to have the letting agent take tenants through the house to improve your chances of organising tenancy well before settlement day.

From the day that the contracts are signed make sure that you insure the house yourself, even before settlement takes place. When you insure it, insure it for what you believe it would cost if you had to replace the house in twelve months time. If you insure only for the cost of replacement today then you haven't considered that the house could increase in value by $10,000 or even more over the next 12 months. If the house burns down in the twelfth month you could be out of pocket. Insurance is not too costly so make sure you cover your assets well. If you can't work out yourself what it would cost then get a rough estimate from a builder, a fairly close estimate should be available almost immediately.

The vendor may request permission to release the deposit you have lodged for the house, which is normally held in a solicitors' trust account. This request will usually come via your own solicitor, so if he is happy that all is in order you should promptly release the deposit. Your deposit, which could be as much as 10 per cent of the purchase price, or about $14,000, is not being used to the greatest advantage for anyone, so you should release it immediately so the vendor can gain some benefit. This gesture of goodwill won't cost you anything, and will be looked on favourably by the vendor, who might need the money to pay off loans to their advantage.

I always advise people not to negotiate directly with the vendor. You might get to know the seller too well and won't feel comfortable offering a lower price. By getting to know the vendor too well, you open the door for emotion to surface. Always treat an agent as the third person and don't tell the agent that you may be willing to go higher if the first offer is not accepted. The risk is that the agent will use this information to recommend that the vendor not accept your offer. After all, he knows you will go higher.

A friend of mine described to me how he made an offer for a house to an agent. He told the agent 'I'll offer $100,000 for the property and won't go any higher than $115,000'. Obviously he bought the property for exactly $115,000. He was proud of his own negotiations.

In Whose Name Should You Buy Property? When you buy investment property you must be careful about whose name you put it under. If both partners are on the same marginal tax rate, buy it in both names. On the other hand, if you are working and earning a very high taxable income but your partner is on a much lower taxable income or even no income at all, then you would buy it in your own name. Your investment will be negatively geared for the first few years so in the event of any loss on the property, the tax office will provide more help to those with the higher marginal tax rate. If there is no income, the tax office gives no help at all.

Where a property has a positive cash flow it should be bought in the name of the taxpayer on the lower rate. Remember that a positive cash flow will be taxed at the marginal rate of the owner.

Although capital gains tax will be hit the hardest in the higher taxpayer's name, don't be too concerned. As an investor you are not looking at selling your properties for years to come and will probably sell only when your income (and therefore your tax rate) is lower.

Always buy your own home in your and your partner's own names and not through a company or trust. Your own home in your name is not liable for capital gains tax, whereas using a trust or company makes your company liable.

Before buying any property or shares it is advisable to see your accountant for advice on this issue. Your accountant can advise when it may be preferable to buy through a company or family trust. It is his or her job to know exactly in which identity you should place your investments and, later on, even your cars. But make sure you ask for advice before you buy, because it is usually too late once they have already been bought.

Don't expect to learn all of these avenues of purchasing yourself. This is why you employ accountants who are specialists in their field, so let them guide you accordingly.

11

BANKS AND MONEY MATTERS

The most suitable type of loan for your needs will be determined by how long you need to pay it off and at which point you would feel comfortable about re-borrowing up to the level of your new equity in the property. That's when you put a deposit on your next investment. Some people are more comfortable paying off the entire loan before starting out again, which is what Mary and I did. However, I certainly would not behave that way now if I were starting all over. Instead, I would pay off say, $30,000, and then immediately re-borrow this for the deposit on the next investment. But on this point, you have to find your own comfort circle and work within it. As you learn more and invest more, you will begin to find that your comfort circle expands all the time, making you more willing to do things differently.

If you can't sleep at night then you are outside your comfort circle, which I have to say would not suit me. I am very conservative and need to feel very secure. I only feel comfortable when I know exactly what I am doing. If you intend to pay off a loan within a couple of years, take out a principal and interest loan with a variable rate of interest. Fixed interest loans usually carry a penalty for early repayment, a restriction you certainly don't want. Should your number one goal be to pay the home loan out as quickly as possible, get down to some serious saving. With every pay, take as much as possible off your loan and spend only the remainder.

And that really works; if you allow only a very small amount each week for spending, then that is all you will spend. How little can you live on each week? Having done your homework and worked it out, try over the course of the year to cut back even more. It is amazing how much you can go without today, when you realise that you can have whatever you like further down the track.

WORKING WITH THE BANKS

A good loans manager can help you find the best loans to increase your profits. The loans you obtain might not necessarily have the cheapest interest rates or fees but they are structured in a flexible way so that you are able to use the equity in your investments to buy more investments.

The more you invest the more you will understand that you want to lessen your taxable income and increase the capital gains on your assets. So in years when you have high depreciation allowances, high franking credits from your share dividends and high expenses, and you have contributed a lot of your income to your own superannuation company, your taxable income will be minimal. Some loans managers would not look favourably on a low taxable income, even though you have had a great year. Your loans manager must be able to understand the accounting papers that you have presented to him, and not just base his views on your final taxable income. If your loans manager at the bank cannot understand your books then find one who can. A good loans manager will help you on your way to financial freedom. An unknowledgeable loans manager will retard your progress.

Even though I have said this, do not expect to receive a loan from the bank if you don't have enough equity for the security of the loan. You must have the equity to secure the loan as well as the cash flow to service the loan. You don't need a lot of cash flow at all to buy an investment property if you have done your purchasing homework very well. Your own private home loan will demand a much greater cash flow.

As you become bigger in the eyes of the bank, you will have access to a personal account manager. This manager will work thoroughly with you and maybe another 20 private clients. He will be contracted with you for a term of say five years and he cannot leave the bank in that time and he will always have you as a private client.

I have had contact with such a private manager and although his service was excellent I found that I could find some loans that better suited me at a different bank. If you are contacted by a personal loans manager then find out exactly what they have to offer but still look around and compare what other banks have to offer as well. Don't think that you have to do all your business with the same bank. At present I do business with seven different financial institutions, but one of these banks has the majority of my business. This might change over the years. Don't assume that you have to be loyal to only one bank. That is not the case.

Our First Personal Home Loan   When I went for our first personal home loan in 1983, you had to have at least $1000 in the bank's account for a term of at least one year or the bank would not give you a loan. These days there are no such criteria. You can walk into any bank and obtain a loan from them if you have the required security.

When I am applying for a loan I will approach every bank in the town and present them with a typed letter. The letter will look something like this.

To the Loans Department,
I have 2 separate loans that are now due for renewal and I am looking around for where to get these properties refinanced.
1. Loan for $166,500 on two units.
2. Loan for $82,800 on a residential house.
The two loans are to be kept separate.
I need information on:
1. Rates of interest for 3, 5, 8 and 10 years for a fixed, interest-only loan.
2. Establishment fees and other loan costs.
3. Solicitor fees if they apply.
4. Amount that I can borrow against the properties.
5. Penalties for paying out the loan early.

6. *Any loans that you feel would be suitable for my investment purposes that are not included in the loans that I have asked for.*

From Sean O'Reilly,

Phone: 5620 0000 or 5620 0001, Mobile: 0408 000 000,

Fax: 5620 0001

You will usually find that the banks will ring you back or fax information to you within the next two days. If they haven't contacted you by the third day then you ring them to see if they wish to submit some figures.

Once all the figures are in front of you, you can work out which banks you want to have a meeting with. I usually end up comparing about three banks and have appointments with each. Do your sums carefully over and over again because if you make a mistake here it can cost you thousands of dollars over the term of the loan.

When you are dealing with three banks you have also bargaining power to your advantage. I make it quite clear that I am comparing one bank with the other.

Fixed vs Variable Interest Rates Some banks might recommend that you should take out a variable rate of interest, which is fine, if the interest rate remains the same or decreases. But what if the interest rates do rise and rise dramatically.

On every loan I obtain I will fix the interest rates. What if the interest rates go back up to say 16 per cent? I will again fix the interest rates on any loans that I refinance but

I am not likely to buy any more property with the interest rates at this level. The money is too dear for me. If the interest rates are at this height then there will be many owners that are finding it difficult to service loans and some will have to sell. At the same time many prospective buyers will be scared off from buying houses as the loans will be too expensive. Therefore we have a situation where there are less buyers. When we have more people wanting to sell and get out, at the same time as we have fewer people wanting to buy we have a very over-supplied market with no demand. When this happens prices have to fall until the buyers and sellers balance out again. The demand for money will be less so the price of money must again fall. I personally would wait until the interest rates decreased to 10 per cent or lower before I would start buying again.

Presenting Your Paper Work When you are looking for finance to finance an investment don't forget that you do not need a lot of savings and often you don't need any savings at all. You might already have enough equity in another property to help with part of the security for your next investment. But before you go to any bank for any loan do a cash flow statement including the property you are seeking a loan for. Have an assets and liabilities statement as well to show the bank exactly your overall equity in all of your properties.

To do a detailed cash flow statement you will need an

estimate of the rent you will receive and the interest paid. You should already know the depreciation allowance that you will be able to claim. (Depreciation allowance is explained in more detail on page 180.) For this exercise, we will use a total of $3000 for rates, insurance and maintenance.

Purchase Price	$115,000
Purchase Costs	$6000
Interest Rate	7.5%
Rent	$160/week
Insurance/Rates/Maintenance	$3000
Depreciation Allowances	$3000

You could obtain a total loan of $115,000 using this property and part of the equity in another property, as security. Because you have enough security you do not have to pay any mortgage insurance.

In this example I assume that you are on the 47 per cent tax bracket and you also have a 1.5 per cent Medicare levy. This combined equals 48.5 per cent.

Loan $115,000 × 7.5% interest = −$8630/year

Rent $160/w × 52 weeks   =   +$8320

Insurance/Rates/Maintenance =   −$3000

Depreciation Allowances   =   −$3000

Total Tax Deductions   =   −$6310

Tax Refund = $6310 × 48.5 per cent = $3060

CASH FLOW = Interest   −$8630

          Rent   +$8320

          Insurance/
          Maintenance/Rates −$3000

Tax refund   +$3060
Cash flow cost
     per year   −$250

Cash flow cost per week = $250 ÷ 52 weeks = $4.81 per week.

So in this example you would be able to give up just two cups of coffee a week to cover your cash flow to buy your investment property.

Change all of the variables in the above example to suit your circumstance and see just how little it will cost you.

In the above example we have used the 48.5 per cent marginal tax rate. Let's see what happens when we use the 30 per cent tax rate which is when your taxable income is between $20,001 and $50,000 a year.

Total Tax Deductions are still   −$6310
Tax refund = $6310 × 30% = $1893
Cash Flow will now be: Interest   −$8625
                       Rent   +$8320
                       Insurance/
                       Rates/
                       Maintenance   −$3000
                       Tax refund   +$1893
Cash flow cost per year   −$1412

Total cost per week = $1412 ÷ 52 weeks = $27.15 per week.

Therefore when you are on the 30 per cent tax rate the house will still only cost you $27.15 in cash flow a week.

When you alter the variables around in the previous example I want you to put in an interest rate of 16 per cent. If you don't fix your interest rate on your loans then this is possible. Don't forget that interest rates were around 18.5 per cent in the late 1980s. Have a look at what this will cost you a year.

The cash flow figures shown above are what you should also present to the loans officer at the bank. Many loan officers will not have any investments in property themselves and will not understand that you need minimal cash flow only to service investment property loans. You can teach your bank manager these basic accounting principles. If you play with the numbers for a short time you will understand them completely.

Make sure that before you buy the next investment the accountant has informed you that you can easily afford the extra cash flow required to service your loan. You do not have to be an educated accountant yourself. This is why these people are here to assist you. As time goes by on your road to wealth you will know yourself when you are able to buy the next investment.

The image that you project to the bank is just as valuable as your skills. When you walk into the bank you must look like you are already a success. Act like you are full of confidence and the bank will take more notice of you. Your first images at the bank are exactly the same as your first images when you go for a job interview. Everyone initially judges everyone else by the first impression that they make.

To increase this self-confidence find a smart suit to wear to your first appointment at the bank. If you know that you look smart this will automatically make you feel more confident. By doing more homework concerning the loans, you will be more confident in understanding what the loans officer is talking about. If you don't know what he is talking about then whatever you do, don't pretend that you do understand. You will come unstuck further down the track. If you don't understand then have him explain it again and in more detail.

I used to always audio tape every appointment with my accountant, solicitor and loans manager. Get yourself a small tape recorder and put it on the table between the two of you. You cannot expect to understand or remember everything that they say. Go home and listen to the tape again immediately with a pen and pad in front of you. If still you are not sure about anything that was discussed ring him again and clarify your misunderstandings. Don't assume that you have to secure your loan on your first appointment. Take your time. You need a lot of time to think over the alternatives.

Your credit rating is important. If you have ever been overdue on paying any accounts, it does not go down well with the lending officer. The bank that you are applying to for a loan, will have a record of other loans that you presently or previously had. The bank will ring these places and see how well you have serviced your loan. You want them to reply that you have never been late on a payment. The bank will ring the credit bureau, which will give details on any loans that you have a bad track record on.

You do not need a credit rating to obtain a loan but it does help as it gives the bank something to look back on to see what history you have. If you don't have a credit rating because you have never borrowed before but you do rent a property then ask for a letter from the real estate agent to state how you have never been late in paying your rent. All of these little things will look favourably on you securing a loan.

Mistakes to avoid We certainly didn't get it right the first time. Our mistakes over the years have cost us thousands of dollars in lost opportunities, especially when it comes to loans.

When Mary and I started to invest we were very naive and because of this we made many mistakes. Nearly every mistake that I have told you not to make, sometime in our investing we made that exact mistake.

When we first started to invest we made every one of our loans a principal and interest loan and we never fixed the interest rate. My aim was to pay each loan off as quickly as possible, which is great when you first begin investing because you decrease your loan and have a positive cash flow coming from your property. Once we achieved this we knew that there was no possible risk at all, but for every extra dollar we were making we were paying a lot in tax. But still we kept on paying more and more off the loan.

Looking back, we would have handled it all very differently. Instead of having every loan principal and interest, we should have had perhaps one principal and interest loan with a variable rate of interest and the others as fixed rate, interest-only loans. Therefore we would still have the ability to decrease our overall risks by paying more off on the principal and interest loan if we wanted to, and as well secure the loan on the other properties by fixing the interest rates at 13.5 per cent, which is what the average rate was at the time.

All of the interest rates on our loans went from 13.5 per cent up to 18.75 per cent very quickly. So yes, we did try to pay them out faster but our cash flow had decreased as it was being eaten up by the interest increases. The best lesson was that we must always fix the interest rates to insure against any interest rate increases.

We found ourselves in a very sticky situation, and had to act fast. We found a financial group that would refinance all of the loans into a five-year fixed, interest-only loan of 15.5 per cent. Yes, the fees were very costly to establish this loan, which also had very high mortgage solicitors' fees, but over a five-year term this was far preferable to paying 18.75 per cent for the next five years with no security against the interest rates rising even more.

What did we do wrong this time? We put all five properties into the one large loan and borrowed only 52 per cent of the value of all of the properties combined. At this time the financial lending group was offering loans up to 70 per cent of valuation so there was a lot of property tied up for the size of the loan that I received. Not being able to use this extra equity was not such a bad thing at the time, as I wouldn't have bought any more properties while money was going to cost me 15.5 per cent.

Another advantage of this loan was that I could pay the interest in advance. For example, if you have a loan of $100,000 and the interest rate for the year is 8.5 per cent and pay all of the interest for the year up front, then you will receive a discount of 0.2 per cent so your interest rate will now be 8.3 per cent. The discount of 0.2 per cent is not the biggest advantage. You have calculated that you have a taxable income which puts you into the top marginal tax bracket, which will be 47 per cent + 1.5 per cent Medicare levy. This calculation has been done well before the end of the financial year, which in Australia is on 30 June. So if you pay your interest ($100,000 × 8.3% = $8300) in advance before the 30th of June then the full $8300 is a tax deduction for that tax year, finishing on the 30th of June. Therefore you would have a tax refund on the $8300 of $8300 × 48.5% = $4026. So therefore your overall costs out of pocket for your interest would be $8300 − $4026 refund = $4274.

One way of minimising your tax is by paying interest on loans in advance. Your accountant will advise you when it is to your advantage to do this. Keep this in mind when you are working with the banks. If you are in a position where you might require the ability to pay interest in advance on your loans then make sure that the bank allows this as part of your loan package.

Therefore your ideal investment loan might be something like this. A five-year, fixed interest rate of 7.8 per cent, interest only, Option to pay interest in advance loan, using a single property as security for each loan.

Because the total loan/valuation ratio for me was 52 per cent, I would have been better off to pull one property out of the loan. There would still be enough security in the properties for the amount of money that was borrowed. This free property would then be fully unencumbered so I could use it further down the track to help purchase other investments, if I wanted to.

KNOW YOUR FINANCIAL LIMITS

Your personal home loan can control your whole investment powers. Many people find that monthly home loan repayments exhaust all of their available money. When you get a home loan your primary goal should be to pay it off immediately. To pay in fortnightly repayments instead of monthly will help to speed repayments but not enough for you. You have to be far more aggressive – you must pay off everything you possibly can, even as much as $600 a week.

Your first goal is to pay into your investment account and to pay money off your house, because to do this is your greatest investment at the moment. Remember also that the first house you buy should be a cheap house. When we bought our first house we paid $44,000 for it at a time when the average price for an average-sized house was about $60,000.

Where there are two wages coming in you will find that you can probably pay three-quarters of total wage income off your loan per week, living on the other quarter for the week. We did this, carefully budgeting day-to-day expenses.

You might have $20,000 in the bank and you want to buy a house worth $140,000. Rather than move on it immediately, you may think it worthwhile to delay for six months while saving another $10,000 to lift the deposit to $30,000. I don't agree with this. The house might also have gone up in price by $10,000 over the next six months as well. When you have done your homework on the overall market and the area in which you plan to live, and have located the house you would be happy with for the next few years you should move in and buy it. I'm not recommending that you rush into buying; on the contrary, you may look and study your market for four months by checking out every house for sale within your price bracket. Just know your financial limit in terms of repayments so that you don't over-extend yourself on the loan.

WHAT LOAN IS BEST FOR YOU?

The price you pay for a house and the position of the house have a great bearing on the amount of profit that you can receive from your investment. But, there is another large factor that will determine the amount of profit that you receive from your investments. This is the type of loan you obtain from the bank.

If you enter the bank and ask for all of the different sorts of loans that the bank offers, you will find that there are so many and it would take you days to read through and have a basic understanding of all of them. It is far better for you to have an idea of the sort of loan you want and then see if the bank can recommend something better. In this section I will explain the difference between some of the loans that are relevant to investing and then I will explain why some loans are better than others and which loan will suit you for which circumstance.

There are two major loans that you will deal with most of the time and there are different variations to both of these loans. The two loans that I will explain in more detail are the **principal and interest loan** and the **interest-only** loan.

Principal and Interest Loans The principal and interest loan will usually be the first one you obtain because this loan gives the bank more security as times go by. Nearly everyone with a personal home mortgage is on a principal and interest loan. Let's assume you have bought your first personal home, and you have paid $100,000 for the house and the bank is willing to give you a loan of 80 per cent. The buying costs were $5000 and you had $25,000 saved.

$100,000	Purchase Price
+$5000	Buying expenses
−$25,000	Cash as a deposit
$80,000	Loan required

The bank gives you a loan of $80,000 but no more, as it is 80 per cent of $100,000 cost price.

You are 25 years old so you get a loan for a term of another 25 years and it is a principal and interest loan. You know that you are going to pay the loan out very quickly so you decide not to fix the interest rate but instead have a variable rate of interest which can, to the bank's discretion, rise or fall. The interest rate for the variable rate is about

7.5 per cent. The bank will calculate your repayments figure for the next 25 years of its term. The figure they would set would be about $600 per month. Of which $500 would be for the interest component and $100 would be paid off the $80,000 principal amount. Because the principal is becoming less with each month's payment you will find that every month a few more dollars of the $600 goes into the principal repayment and thus a few less dollars are required for the interest component. In the first few years most of the payment is for interest and very little is for the principal payments. In the last few years of the loan it is the other way around, very little interest is left to pay and the balance of the $600 comes off the principal.

Because it is a principal and interest loan with a variable rate of interest you are allowed to pay as much off the loan as you like whenever you like to speed up the whole proceedings. This is why you want this sort of loan as it is your personal home and the interest is not tax deductible so you are in a hurry to pay out as much as you can, as soon as possible.

If you don't want to have a variable interest rate loan but instead fix the interest rate for three years then you are not allowed to pay off anymore of the principal other than the monthly repayments unless you are willing to pay a penalty which can be quite expensive. Therefore to fix your interest rate on this loan is not for you. If you are not going to pay any extra off your personal home, other than the monthly repayments, then you are far better off to fix the interest on your loan for maybe a five-year term. This means that if interest rates go up in general then you don't have to worry about them as yours are still fixed at the initial rate. After the five years of the fixed rate have expired then you can revert back to a variable rate and then start paying off more of your loan, which will now not require a penalty payment.

You would not use a principal and interest loan for an investment loan because the interest part of the payment is tax deductible but the principal part of the payment is not. Also by paying off the principal amount each week you are tying up cash that could be used on a deposit for your next investment.

Interest-only loans Interest-only loans should be used for investment purposes, as you don't want to pay any extra money off the loan at all but instead use it for your next investment. The title of the loan is self-explanatory. You only pay the interest on the borrowed funds and you do not pay anything off the principal itself.

I would use a principal and interest loan for an investment only when it is your first property and you are still living at home. In this case you will want to pay off some of the loan until you are very comfortable and then you can invest in your next property. Your next property would be an interest-only loan. Another time you can use a principal and interest loan is when you are comfortable that you have enough investments and you are happy to pay off some of your debt. This is similar to a loan that I received in 1999 where I obtained a principal and interest loan over a 24-year term with the interest fixed for 10 years at 7.5 per cent. I felt that interest rates were on the move upwards so

I was more relaxed in fixing it for the 10 years even if it meant that I had to pay some principal off also. By fixing it for the 10 years I believe that I was minimising any risk, which is what investing is all about. The amount of principal that I will pay off during the 10 years of a fixed rate, will be minimal but increasing each year.

After the term of an interest-only loan, which might be a term of five years, you have to negotiate the loan with the same bank or a different bank, so you will have new fees to pay for the establishment again. This is not the case for a principal and interest loan because you could have a term of say 25 years so you don't necessarily have to look around for a bank to refinance the loan once your first five years is completed.

Part Fixed and Part Variable Loans   Let's assume that you have a personal home loan of $100,000 and you know that within the next three years you will have $50,000 of this loan paid out but no more. Why not split your loan into two parts? Divide the loan into $50,000 principal and interest loan with a variable rate of interest and $50,000 as an interest only loan with a fixed rate of interest. This means that you can maintain flexibility of the principal and interest loan, and at the same time have a degree of protection from future interest rate rises. You can now pay off the principal and interest component part of the loan as quickly as you want to without penalties, and at the same time if the interest rates rise you don't have to worry as you have already locked the interest rate in at the initial rate, on the fixed interest component of the loan.

All of the fees and the interest rates can be negotiated so that is why you must go to about five banks each time you refinance so you can see who will give you the best deal. If you stay with the same bank and don't even look at the other banks, then this same bank will offer you what it wants to offer you and not necessarily what is best for you. The banks are trying to sell you money for the best price that they can get. You are trying to buy money for the cheapest possible price that you can get. Make sure you bargain with the banks. I have come across the situation where the total cost difference of a loan from two different banks was over $10,000. This was for a term of five years so it would have cost me $2000 a year more if I selected the wrong bank.

What are the Costs?   Different banks will charge you different interest rates but they will also charge you different fees. You must add up all of the fees and work out what the loan will cost you for the entire term of the loan. You will then compare this with other banks and make sure that it is for the same type of loan.

Some banks will charge you an establishment fee of up to $700 while other banks will not charge you establishment fees at all. With some banks there are mortgage solicitors' fees that can amount up to $2000 a loan, while other banks include their in-house solicitors' fees as part of the establishment fee. Different rates are charged for valuation fees as well. If you own a share discount card with a bank there could be discounts on some of the fees.

If you pay an upfront fee of say $300 to some banks then

you can also obtain discounts on most other upfront fees and ongoing fees. Some discounts offer 0.5 per cent off the standard home loan rate of interest or up to 50 per cent off loan-establishment fees. This is why you have to look around and not just go to the one bank for a loan. If you do your own homework you can save thousands of dollars. It might cost you a full two days of research but if it saves you thousands of dollars then you are being paid well for your time.

The borrowing costs of an investment loan, which do not include the costs to purchase the house, are all tax deductible. The total borrowing costs include: the stamping of the mortgage; the establishment fee; the mortgage solicitors' fee; the house valuation fee; registration fees; and the mortgage insurance fee. You might not need mortgage insurance. Assume these fees total $2200. These costs are deductable over the term of the loan so if the loan is a five-year, fixed, interest-only loan then the $2200/5 years = $440 is deductible each year.

Provide protection

Fixed Interest Costs In all interest-only loans I fix the interest rate for a period of five years so that I know if rates rise dramatically then I am still paying out exactly the same interest. If interest rates fall then I will be paying more than the new lesser rate and I see this as part of an insurance cover, in case they rose dramatically. I look at it as if the interest rate is at present 7.5 per cent then it could rise over the next five years to a rate of say 15 per cent, where if it is going to fall it is more likely to just fall one or two percentage points down to 5.5 per cent. To me the choice of not fixing the interest rates is far too risky. A risk that I am not comfortable in having. Every one of my property loans has the interest rate fixed for a five- or 10-year term. To fix the interest rate gives you the ability to budget ahead for the purpose of other investments. A fixed interest rate for five years will usually be higher than the variable rate but it is still worth paying this extra as an insurance measure.

Loans – Be Wary   The bank will ask you to put all of your properties with them as the more security they have the happier they are. If the bank asks you to put two or more properties together to be covered by the one loan then don't do it. If you want to sell one of these properties or change it over to a different sort of loan then you have to negotiate a new loan for all of the properties. This will add to your costs and create a lot more work. By having one property with each loan, you have more flexibility to do what you want with each individual property.

Many loans have a penalty if you want to alter them before the fixed interest rate has completed its term. So if you have two properties with the one loan but you only want to alter the loan for the purpose of selling one property, you will be penalised for the whole loan.

A loan document is very scary to most people and also very long but as an investor it is your job to learn how to understand a loan document. Read them diligently and if you are not sure about something then whatever you do, ask someone about it. Your solicitor can read over it if you wish and then inform you that everything is in order but he might not pick up that the interest rate has been fixed for three years when you wanted if fixed for five years. Only you know what you have discussed with the bank officer.

The loans officer at the bank might also tell you that you are far better off putting your money in one of the bank's managed funds rather than for you to invest in property. What experience has this loans officer got in investing himself? This is where your own homework will pay very good dividends for you. The more you know, the sooner you will win the game. Actually I personally do not put any money into any managed funds anymore as I found the returns I was making on two funds that I had money in were nowhere near what I was making through my property and share investments. I once had a loans officer telling me that I was silly if I thought I could make money out of negative gearing property. I thanked him for his advice and went to another bank.

How Much Can You Borrow?   The size of a loan for an investment property will be determined by two main factors.
1. The bank will usually give you 80 per cent of your equity and,
2. How much can you borrow so that your cash flow will cover your expenses comfortably?

Never become over-committed. If you find that you are having trouble servicing the loan on one property then whatever you do don't think that by buying a second property it will become any easier. It won't. It will become worse and often it will get you into very deep water. This is where people become over-committed and have to sell at whatever price the buyer is offering. You will go backwards very quickly if you ever get into this situation.

If you find that you are having trouble servicing one loan then you have to take action and pay out as much of that loan as possible so that your interest expenses lessen. If you do believe that you have done everything possible to lessen the pressure of payments but are still no better off after six months then you have to take drastic action and sell something so that your cash flow improves. You might sell a car or an investment home and consolidate for at least a year, before you start to look at doing some form of investing again.

Don't forget, if you can't have a relaxing sleep at night because of money worries, then you have over-extended yourself and need to drop back a bit. When you fix your interest rate and have loans that are interest-only loans then your cash flow will become better and therefore you will be able to budget a lot better and maybe relax more.

Will You Ever Own Your Investment If You Get interest-only loans? How many people have wondered how a loan works if you never pay it off? I definitely did. Let's look at it this way. Today, you buy an investment property worth $140,000 and you have a $110,000 loan, which is an interest-only loan fixed for five years. When the five years expire you will again fix it for another five years and pay the interest only again. At the moment your goal is to build wealth which means, don't pay off the loans if you have the cash flow to service them. In 15 years' time, with a capital appreciation of 9 per cent a year the $140,000 house will now be worth $510,000 and your loan will still only be $110,000 so now your equity in this house will be $510,000 − $110,000 = $400,000. As an investor you would have progressively used this growing equity in this house to buy more investments.

Never Go Guarantor If your best friends approach you and ask you to go guarantor for them with respect to a loan they want to obtain, say 'no'. You are being asked for much more than your friendship, or just a few thousand dollars.

You must understand that the guarantor signs a legal guarantee that they will help the owners of the property service the loan, and that if this does not happen the bank can take the guarantor's house as security over the loan. How bad would this be if your friends decide to go to England on the very day that the bank rings you. You could be servicing your best friends' home with no way out of it.

If you want to help your friends, you would be far better off lending them money – but with a written contract. Charge a reasonable interest rate and insist that the loan is paid out over the next 12 months, with monthly repayments. Do not give them 12 months with payment at the end. Do not give them a loan without a contract. You would be asking for trouble.

I won't lend money to any family member or friend because if something goes wrong I will lose a good friend as well as my money. I can be of far more help by working with them and the bank, showing them how they can manage to get a loan

MORTGAGE OFFSET ACCOUNTS

Most financial institutions now have mortgage offset accounts which help homeowners finance their own homes in a more tax-effective way. If $8000 is deposited in a normal bank account at 5 per cent per annum it would earn $400 in interest. But for those in the top tax bracket, almost half would be eaten up in tax, leaving earnings of $200 from the $8000 deposit. If their home loan was $100,000 at 8 per cent, it would cost $8000 interest per annum. Over the year, they would be out of pocket by $7800 ($8000 – $200).

On the other hand, a mortgage offset account charges interest only on the difference between your home loan and the balance in the deposit account.

So the $8000 in an offset mortgage account, would mean the interest is charged only on the outstanding amount, that is $92,000 ($100,000 – $8000). The interest bill for the year would then be $7360 ($92,000 × 8%). The difference between placing $8000 in a normal deposit account and using an offset account would be $440 ($7800 – $7360). It may seem like a small amount but remember, you are just saving and investing one dollar at a time to become financially free.

You may find that offset accounts are different at each bank so shop around.

ASSET BUILDER ACCOUNTS

The house I previously lived in was built in 1987, and from the time we began planning to build it, I opened an account to be used solely for that purpose, directing any income I received into it. When this account grew to about $15,000 I transferred the money to a six-month term deposit account paying a higher rate of interest. Then I resumed saving into the initial 'house' account.

From the time I began using the savings account up until we had paid the last instalment on the house was about 13 months later; we had no loan at all for the house. It was fully paid for by the time it was completed. During this period I stopped paying off the principal on our business loan. This was done because the interest on the business loan was tax deductible, whereas the interest on any loan for our private home would bring no tax benefit at all. Our goal therefore was to keep interest payments low by obtaining the smallest possible loan for our home, a goal we achieved by avoiding the need for any loan (or interest) at all.

In 1995 I worked out that I was not using the equity in our then own private house at all and that this was not a good investment strategy. At the time one bank was offering an 'asset builder' account, a kind of old-style overdraft account using your property as security. This home was valued at $200,000, against which the bank gave us an asset builder account with a limit of $160,000 (80 per cent of the $200,000 valuation). I now had a facility similar to a cheque account; I could write out cheques for any amount up to $160,000.

It cost us about $700 to establish the account, which had no on-going management fees and a variable interest rate. This was calculated daily so that, if I write a cheque for $20,000, interest is charged only on that amount, and if $10,000 is paid back into the account, the interest on this $10,000 stops on that day. I pay interest only on the balance owed at any particular time.

Now, if I see an investment property I want to buy I know I can get a deposit immediately by writing a cheque from the asset builder account, and – because the account is used only for business purposes – the interest I pay is fully tax deductible. I might also decide to buy say $20,000 worth of shares using money from this account, and with that $20,000 I could also borrow another $20,000 from the share broker through margin lending (discussed later). In that way, I could borrow the full $40,000 to buy shares without using any of my own money.

Once your investment portfolio begins to grow substantially you may think about buying some personal items, such as a car. Let's assume you buy a car for $60,000, and – because you have no money in deposit accounts – you write a cheque against your asset builder account. Since the car is for personal use, interest on the $60,000 loan is not tax deductible, which definitely is not what you want as an investor.

This situation can be altered. Look at your share portfolio and find shares which have had a good run with little prospect of much more capital gain. Sell these and pay the money into the asset builder account. The car then has no finance costs. Of course, there might be a delay of a couple of months from the time the car is bought until I feel it is the right time to sell the shares, but a couple of months won't matter. You will be paying interest on the $60,000 for only a couple of months, about $800 in fact ($60,000 × 8% × two months ÷ 12 months), not a great deal of money.

The next step might now be some months later when you see a share you believe is at a discount to its present and future worth. You can now buy these shares with the $60,000 from the asset builder account to return your share portfolio to its previous value. Bear in mind that it is the purpose of the loan that determines whether or not interest payments are tax deductible. The loan for the private car was not tax deductible because it was for private use, while the loan to buy shares was for investment purposes and is therefore tax deductible.

These are two different scenarios, even though they were transacted through the same asset builder account – secured against the home in which you live. During the past five years the asset builder account has been of great comfort to me. The knowledge that $160,000 is available to spend at any time gives me great flexibility, and a way to deal with the situation if I should calculate something wrongly somewhere in my investments. It's also a comfort to know that if the stock market has a substantial correction I have $160,000 to throw at the market immediately. I can watch shares and not have to worry about where to obtain money to make a quick purchase; the account acts like a buffer to which I can turn if required.

Because of my conservative views I have never borrowed

anywhere near the $160,000 available to me and most of the time the account has a zero balance. I use it more as a back-up account. Other people might use an asset builder account or the equity in their own home in a very different way, perhaps using it not for investments but to buy personal items, such as jewellery, a boat, car or holidays. By doing this, these people are building roadblocks in the middle of their road to financial independence. We face enough difficulties in our lives without creating more for ourselves, and self-inflicted roadblocks are always difficult to remove when we wake up to ourselves and try to find a smoother path to financial freedom.

Helping Your Own Children If I want to help my own children begin investing I will be very willing to use equity in my own properties to help secure a loan for an investment home for them. For instance, if one of my children had saved $16,000 and wanted to buy a first investment home for $120,000, I would be happy to provide sufficient equity in one of my properties to enable the bank to increase the amount they would be willing to lend. It would work this way.

Once my child paid for loan and purchase costs, the sum of $126,000 would be required, and the bank would be happy to lend $96,000 ($120,000 × 80%). Because $16,000 has already been saved, there is now a shortfall of $14,000 ($126,000 required minus bank loan $96,000 and $16,000 saved). So by giving equity in my own properties to the value of $20,000, the bank would have plenty of security, amounting to as much as $16,000 ($20,000 × 80%), whereas only $14,000 is actually required. This is one of the best ways to help your children start investing.

If my children were about 20 years old and still living at home when buying their first investment property I would persuade them to make as their first goal paying off part of their first investment loan to provide equity for a deposit on a second property.

NEGATIVE GEARING – IT CAN WORK FOR YOU

So far in the book I have touched on the subject of negative gearing but as it is such a great tool it needs a more detailed explanation. The Australian tax laws, through negative gearing, allow for the expenses on an income-producing property to be deducted from other taxable income. This lessens the tax liability. At the same time, the investments that we are negatively gearing should appreciate in value, thus generating capital growth.

You can negatively gear any investments by borrowing to finance the purchase of these investments. To negatively gear means that the interest on borrowings exceed the income derived from the investment. I negatively geared both property and shares, but most of my investments are now positively geared which means that the income now exceeds the expenses. I now have a positive cash flow with most of these investments.

Do not negatively gear investments that will not have

reasonable capital growth. Don't believe that because you are negatively gearing and thus saving tax that you are doing well. The tax saving is not the only thing you have to consider. The investment must be a good investment first, and the tax saving can then be looked at as a bonus.

Some people believe that if they make a loss of say $10,000 on an investment, then the government will pay all of this loss through tax refunds. This is not the case. The tax refund paid back to you will be determined by the marginal rate of tax that you are paying. So if you are presently earning between $6001 and $20,000 taxable income, then your marginal tax rate will be only 17 per cent. So therefore the tax refund that you receive will be $10,000 × 17 per cent = $1700. You will still have to find the other ($10,000 − $1700 refund = $8300) yourself. Table 11.1 will show you what you will have to find to pay out of your own pocket. It depends on your marginal tax rate.

Table 11.1

$ TOTAL LOSS COSTS	$ TAXABLE INCOME	% MARGINAL TAX	$ YOUR OUT-OF-POCKET COSTS
10,000	Up to $6,000	Nil	$10,000
	$6,001 to $20,000	17	$8,300
	$20,001 to $50,000	30	$7,000
	$50,001 to $60,000	42	$5,800
	Excess over $60,000	47	$5,300

You can see that the higher the marginal tax rate that you are on, the less you have to pay out of your pocket, so therefore, the more beneficial negative gearing is to you.

When you buy a property that is going to be negatively geared, it is far better to buy it in the name of the partner who has the highest taxable income. The higher earners get the biggest tax breaks. When you first buy your investment property you might borrow for the full purchase price say $110,000 plus the purchasing costs $6000. You will only be able to do this when you have extra equity in another property. You will need this equity and the security of your new investment property for the overall security of the loan.

In the beginning your interest expenses will be very high as you are borrowing the whole amount. Therefore you would class yourself as highly geared. Your loan/value ratio could look like this.

Loan = 116
Value = 110 = 105%
Loan/Value ratio = 116 ÷ 110 = 105%

This means you are 105 per cent geared on your property.

As the years pass you will find that the property will increase in value but the loan will remain the same. Let us assume that the capital growth on the house over the next five years averages at 7 per cent. The house in five years time will be worth $154,281.

$110,000 × 1.07% = 1. $117,700
2. $125,939
3. $134,755

4. $144,188

5. $154,281

Your loan value ratio will now have decreased to 116 ÷ 154 = 75 per cent.

During these five years your rent will also increase so that the income from the property will increase and therefore your overall losses on the property will decrease. As time goes by, income from the property will equal your total property deductions. Now you no longer have negative gearing. In the next few years you will have a positive cash flow. This profit from the investment property will now have tax taken out of it at your marginal tax rate. However, you would probably have bought another investment by now using the new equity in your investment as part of the security. You would again be back in the position of negative gearing.

When you are negatively gearing a property you are carrying costs at first but these costs must be compensated by the capital growth in the property. If the property does not increase in value over time, there would be no use in putting your own money into the investment when you have this negative cash flow.

Negative gearing will allow for potentially higher returns on your investment but it can also involve a higher risk if it is not used correctly. Many people believe that it is very costly to invest in property and, yes, they will be correct if they buy the wrong house at the wrong time and use the wrong loan. The type of loan that you obtain will also depend on your own investment strategies. Your aim in investing in property is that you want property with good capital growth. This sometimes means that the rent income return on your property could be quite low. This rent return is called gross return.

It is more important for your property to have good capital growth than to have high rental return. If you can achieve high capital growth and high rental returns at the same time well then that is great. But if you have high capital growth but only low rental returns well this is fine too. When you have rental returns that are less than the interest expenses on your loan and the other running expenses, then the negative gearing will give you a very valuable tax refund to help pay for these expenses. You have both the tenant and the taxman helping you pay the interest on your loans. With your own private house you have to pay back the loan entirely by yourself.

With an interest-only loan you will not pay off any of your loan. The way you will make your money is by the property increasing in value as the market increases in value and the rent on the property will increase every year also. After a few years your negatively geared property will become positively geared because the rents will constantly increase. You must learn to understand exactly what negative gearing is. Most people know about it and know that it is happening but have no idea how it exactly works. Make it your job to understand negative gearing completely as it will help you make a lot of money.

Tax Deductions in Different Marginal Tax Brackets The greater the deductions from a loss on your property the more your taxable income decreases and then some of your deductions are likely to come out of a lower marginal tax bracket. When this happens the less refund you get per dollar deduction as you go from one marginal rate to the lower marginal rates. Let me explain.

Peter is an employee with a taxable income of $61,000. He owns two properties and the total loss on these properties is $17,000. Therefore Peter now has a taxable income of $44,000

$$\begin{array}{r} \$61,000 \\ -\$17,000 \\ \hline \$44,000 \end{array}$$

This $17,000 comes off his employee income so the tax he saves will become less as the amount of $17,000 comes out of the three marginal brackets. The top $1000 is in the above $60,000 bracket which is at 47 per cent, so savings = $1000 × 47% = $470. The next $10,000 is in the $50,001 to $60,000 bracket which is at 42 per cent, so $10,000 × 42% = $4200. The final $6000 is in the $20,001 to $50,000 bracket which is at a rate of 30 per cent, so $6000 × 30% = $1800. So the total tax refund will be:

$$\begin{array}{r} \$470 \qquad (47\%) \\ +\ \$4200 \qquad (42\%) \\ +\ \$1800 \qquad (30\%) \\ \hline \$6470 \end{array}$$

Therefore the total out of pocket from the $17,000 loss will be $17,000 − $6470 = $10,530.

His $61,000 income subtracting $17,000 Investment loss then looks like this.

$$\$17,000 = \begin{array}{ll} \$1,000 \times 47\% = & \$470 \\ \$10,000 \times 42\% = & \$4,200 \\ \underline{\$6,000} \times 30\% = & \underline{\$1,800} \\ \underline{\$17,000} & \underline{\$6,470} \end{array}$$

Peter will be out of pocket a total amount of $10,530 ($17,000 − $6470).

If Peter was earning $77,000 instead then the whole investment loss of $17,000 would be in the above $60,000 bracket, so the refund on the $17,000 loss, would be $17,000 × 47% = $7990.

Peter would be out of pocket this time for $9010 ($17,000 − $7990).

This shows that negative gearing is more advantageous to those on a higher taxable income. Don't despair if you have found it hard to follow the above example. This is where you must play with your calculator. It may take some time. Don't give up.

Depreciation and How it Works There are parts of your investment house that you can claim depreciation on. Fixtures and fittings depreciate in value and as an investor you can claim depreciation on these items as a tax deduction. You can also claim depreciation of the building element of your investment property. The amount that you can claim depends on when construction commenced on the house. If the building was constructed between 18 July

1985 and 16 September 1987 then you can claim 4 per cent depreciation. If it was constructed after 15 September 1987 you can claim 2.5 per cent of the cost of the building. You cannot claim for the property value.

Your fixtures and fittings that you are allowed to claim depreciation on will be the carpets, curtains, hot water system, heater etc. You will be able to obtain a list of depreciable items and the amount that you are able to depreciate them, from your accountant. When you depreciate the fixtures and fittings and the building, you are not actually out-laying money. They are not costing you each year but you are still entitled to receive a tax deduction.

Let's assume that the property that you have just bought was built in 1990 and it cost $100,000 to build. On houses built in 1990 the depreciation allowance on buildings was 2.5 per cent so you may claim $100,000 × 2.5% = $2500 for building depreciation. The fixtures and fittings at the time that you bought the house were worth $10,000 so you can claim about 15 per cent of this per year. The actual rate will vary and your accountant will work out the exact rates for you.

$10,000 × 15% = $1500

Your total depreciable items will be:

$2500 building
$1500 fixtures and fittings
$4000 Total depreciation deductions

Don't Over Gear You yourself, with the help of your accountant, will be able to determine when your negative gearing has become too risky. You must be able to find the money that you need for the cash flow, to service your loans.

Make sure you never buy too much and borrow too high so that you are going to get yourself into trouble. If you find that you can't service all of your loans then the bank will make you sell a property so that you reduce your debt. This is known as a fire sale and the bank is not concerned if you don't get the best price for the property, as long as they receive their money back. This is not a good position to be in. You must minimise your risks by not making your loan/value ratio too high. It is far better for you to pay tax and accept a lower overall return on your money, than to become over-committed with no way out.

You might believe that you could just keep on borrowing and buying more and more investments. This is not the case. You must be able to easily service all of the loans. Make sure that you always have more than enough income from your own personal exertion and from your investments so you can always service the loans. You can never be short on cash flow. You must find the right amount of gearing for you. It is better for you to take a more conservative approach at the beginning and as your understanding of gearing improves you will find that you can judge exactly what amount of gearing is best for you. Everyone has their own level of gearing that they are comfortable with.

If you hear of a business going into receivership it is usually because it has become over-committed and can't keep up to its loan repayments. It has often borrowed too much in the first place.

PART 3

Building An
Investment
Portfolio

12

FINANCIAL EDUCATION

How many people do you know who have bought a residential investment property and then lost money on it? How many people do you know who have bought shares and have now seen their portfolio decrease in value to at least half? Why has this happened to these people? In most cases it is because they have not learned about their investment before they executed their purchase. They should have invested in learning about investing and then purchased the asset. They definitely learned something from that mistake.

It is amazing how the lesson is always so much more concrete when we lose money, in comparison to when we make money. Every one of us has the choice to expand our knowledge but very few take up this offer. You have probably heard the saying, 'knowledge is power'. I want to add a bit more to that saying, 'the use of knowledge is power', or 'knowledge is only potential power'.

Many people have the knowledge but just don't use it. If you haven't the financial knowledge and someone else does then you may lose your money to him. It is a Game. If you know more about playing the game then you will win. If your opponent knows more about the game then you will lose.

The more you know about the game of investing, the less you will worry. You must become an 'expert' in the game of money and the only way you will do this is by first increasing your knowledge and to keep on increasing this knowledge. The average person says, 'I know enough about investing'. The expert investor says, 'I don't know enough. I must keep learning'. To be aware of your ignorance and to accept it is the first step toward knowledge.

The average person struggles financially because they take most of their financial advice from other people that are not financially educated. This is often from their parents who have struggled financially themselves. This is where you can help yourself, your children and your grandchildren. The more financially educated you become and the more you teach your siblings the better lifestyle everyone will have. You will be able to teach them what you have learned.

Your biggest asset ever will be your financial education. This asset can never be taken away from you and it will help you with every other asset that you buy. So how do you get that financial education?

EDUCATION BEGINS ONCE YOU LEAVE SCHOOL

Mark Twain said, 'Never let schooling interfere with your education'. Most school report cards will look something like this:

Maths	Pass
English	Pass
Art	Pass
Australian History	Pass

What subject is missing?

Money	FAIL

Why weren't we taught more about financial matters at school?

In what subject was I told that I should never borrow to buy a car?

In what subject was I told to never borrow for non-income-producing products?

Where was I told that I should never use a credit card unless I knew I would have the money available to pay it off by the due date?

Schools teach us how to read, write and do mathematics as the basic, core subjects. There are many other subjects that you can choose to do as you advanced through the system. The general aim of most schools is to teach the students what they need to survive once they leave school. The school prepares them for the workforce. It teaches them how to get a good, secure job or how to extend their education even further by going on to tertiary studies. It is as if the career is their final goal.

We, as parents, are also guilty of promoting that scenario of getting a good education so you can then go out and get a good job. The scary thing is that many people do not like their job. I'm not saying that I am against the school system at all. I was a teacher and I loved what I did and I believed in what I taught. It is amazing how proactive schools are now with new subjects being introduced into the school curriculum. But, where is the financial education?

We teach people how to find a job so that they can earn an income, but do we teach them what is the best thing to do with their money once they receive it? Financial education should be introduced as an addition to all of the great subjects being taught. So, where do you find the information you need?

The most valuable asset you can ever have is knowledge. How many people have a library membership? How many of these people have actually been to the library in the last few months? The library has many great finance books. I personally prefer to buy my own investment books because then I can underline, draw on them, and always refer back to them. I hesitate to lend my books to anyone, as this is my library of knowledge. Most of my notes are in my books. My library is one of my most valuable investments. If someone is really serious in learning about financial investments then it will be far more beneficial for them if they buy their own books. I find it amazing how anyone could think that a $29 investment book is too expensive. That same book has probably just helped me establish a new loan, which saves me $1000 a year for five years. This is an excellent investment. How much more will it save me in years to come?

I have bought literally hundreds of cassettes over the years. I can listen to them over and over again. Initially, I might understand 20 per cent of the information and only remember half of it. So each time I listen I will learn more and more.

I go to all the seminars that I feel are relevant to my goals. Some of these seminars have been great. It is uncanny how sometimes the information that comes from a book or a seminar is exactly the information that I am looking for. Many of these seminars have cost thousands of dollars to attend. I see them as investments and not as expenses. I know people that have told me that the investment seminars are too expensive and so they wouldn't go. These people are still working because they need the money. If you can find free seminars then they are usually a good source of information. Even if these seminars just confirm something that you already know, this confirmation is worth getting.

I buy every newspaper that has a money section in it. I buy the *Personal Investor* magazine and other finance magazines when they have articles in them that I am interested in reading. Every time your bank offers a financial adviser to discuss your investment strategies then it is worth getting their opinions as well. You do not have to put any of your money in their funds. The banks are offering this as a free service.

You must educate yourself. You must study the ways and means that other people have followed to become successful. You must become a student of success. Your mentors will be your teachers. When the student is ready, the teacher will appear. An education is something a person gets for himself. It is not something that someone gives you. You must go out and source your own knowledge through every possible avenue. By reading about how others have been successful in investing, you can learn a great deal about your own investment strategies. All you need to do is learn one lesson from all of the finance books that you read. You only need to gain one insight for it to be worthwhile. By reading all of these books and listening to tapes you can acquire a general idea of the qualities that have helped other people become successful investors. Most investors have the traits of patience, perseverance and determination. They know what they are after and they are determined to get it.

By learning about losses that people have made in investing, you can avoid them. Many people have gone through the same struggle before you and succeeded, and so can you.

From studying those people who have become financially independent it is obvious that as well as acquiring great wealth they must also be able to manage this wealth. To own a large investment portfolio is not enough. Many people have made great fortunes, which have been squandered through mismanagement. Therefore the continuous development of money management skills becomes essential. Without a financial education your money will soon disappear.

A MENTOR: YOUR OWN PRIVATE TEACHER

The best form of education that you can find is by way of a mentor but unfortunately these mentors are hard to find and once found a teacher/pupil relationship is hard to form. If you want to go somewhere, then it is best to find someone who has already been there. If you want to sky-dive it is best that you learn about it from someone who has done it before you. Unfortunately, this is not what we do when we want to know about financial matters. We usually ask someone who has not had the investment success that we are looking for. They are not 'experts' in financial matters.

When our children go to school we are very concerned about whom they play with and who are their peers. You know that most children will become very much like those they play with. Who are your peers? Apart from your family, look at the five people that you spend most of your time with. They could be friends, workers or from an organisation that you are involved in. Put those five people out there in front of you against the wall. Look at them carefully. You are looking in the mirror of the future. What you see is what you will become.

Now from looking in this mirror are you happy or does it scare you? Are you happy with where you are going, what are you doing with your life? This exercise is not about judging other people. This exercise is about judging yourself. Are you happy with the road that you are taking? Your friends might be very happy with their lives, the way they are, and that is great. A person who is content with their life is very fortunate. They have found exactly what they want. I like having people around me who are smarter than me. I like listening to what they have to say.

Be willing to learn from other people. Never believe that you know more than what people have got to offer. If you do this then something will bring you back to earth very quickly. If your ego takes over you will go backwards very quickly. Instead of believing that you can do something on your own seek advice from the experts that are around you. Don't for one minute think that you will one day have learned enough about finance for the rest of your life. Learning how to make money work for you is a lifetime study. It will never end.

I often tell people that if you want to be a millionaire then make sure that the person you are getting the advice from is a millionaire or well on the way to becoming a millionaire. Your adviser must have done it for himself and have the investments to show it.

Find out how many investments and what investments he owns. Does he have to work 60 hours a week because he has to find the money to help himself keep his liabilities? Can he take next month or next year off and still have the income coming in so he can continue on spending the same amount without dipping into his savings? If he can't take time off then he is in exactly the same position as the employee working for someone else, but he is probably worse off. The busier he gets, the more money he might make but also the more he is tied to the office.

There are many so-called 'experts' out there that have become financial advisers and they have the certificate to prove it. How good are these advisers? What sort of return are they receiving from their investments? Some advisers out there will have little idea on how to run their own finances so they will find it hard to show you how you should invest yourself. The adviser's office might look new and he or she is dressed in a very impressive suit, but how do you find out how successful he or she is? You just ask.

Ask what investments he or she might have. Do they own investment property? Where do they own these properties? What shares do they own? An adviser that doesn't own shares would not be suitable for me.

Your Adviser Is An Investment   I hear people say that their adviser only charges them $80 an hour so why would they go to someone who charges $150 an hour. For excellent advisers who can help you become financially free, do not worry about their fees. They will always make a lot more for you than what they will ever charge you.

If your advisers are true professionals then all of their advice should make you good money. A good financial adviser will provide you with information but at the same time he must help to educate you in the areas of financial management. It is their job to teach you what they know. What I pay my financial adviser or my broker is a very small amount in comparison to what money they have made for me.

I am leveraging my own time by paying these advisers to help me make more money. Many of their jobs I do not want to do myself. They can do most of the research for me. They help me leverage my own money and my own time. This is similar to doing maintenance work at my investment houses. Why would I want to fix the washers on the taps myself when I can pay someone who is an expert to do it? I can make more money elsewhere or just do what I want to with that time.

Your financial adviser will see opportunities that you are not aware of. It is their business to do that.

Many advisers receive a commission from the organisations where they invest your money. If one organisation pays the adviser a greater commission than another then why wouldn't the adviser be biased toward this better position. This position might not necessarily be the best position for the investor.

Some advisers will promote managed funds as the best place to put your money, as this is where they will receive their commission. I believe that you can do a lot better yourself if you buy the shares or property directly rather than having someone else manage your money for you. With managed funds there is often an entry fee and an annual management fee that will eat into your profits. You can easily beat the returns on most managed funds. Although this might be the case you might still be more comfortable in putting your money into a managed fund. If so, your adviser will inform you which managed fund is best for you.

At the same time that you are receiving advice you should also be doing your own research on your investments and on future investments. You should also be reading up on what strategies your accountant is using so you can understand exactly where you are financially. Therefore you will be able to do a lot of the groundwork yourself and your accountant/adviser will now advance to the next step. This is a continuous journey of always learning and advancing.

You must realise that to be successful you need the help of others. You cannot do it all yourself. Do you know someone who has done very well in his investments and is now financially free? Ask this person who he has advising him. How did he find this person? Is he happy with this adviser or is he looking for someone better? Ask everyone who you know are investors, who they use for an adviser.

The Time it Cost Me Not to Get Advice Never get too confident. Always assume that you need help in financial matters. When I bought a shop I made a lot of mistakes that cost me a lot of money. At the time the main thing on my mind was that if I ring my adviser and my solicitor it will cost me money. I should have looked at it the other way around. It should have been viewed as, if I ring my solicitor and financial adviser it will be money well spent.

I went to an auction to buy a shop. At this point I did not seek any advice at all. I was the winning bidder and I paid the deposit of 10 per cent and signed the papers. That evening I had a phone call from a gentleman who said that he wanted to buy the shop from me and he would pay $30,000 more to me than what I bought it for. My first reaction was that I had just made $30,000 in less than 24 hours. I then asked myself, 'If I can make $30,000 in one day then imagine what I can make in say two years?' I thanked him for the offer but said no thanks.

About three months later the shop became vacant. The tenants moved, so now I had an empty shop. It took me about six months to find a good tenant, so in these six months I had loan repayments but no rent. That really hurt.

I should have sold the shop when I was offered $30,000 more for it. I could then have looked around and found another shop that I believed was undervalued, and bought it. I should also have seen a solicitor before I even bought the shop and he would have found out that the tenant was not going to stay in the shop for anymore than three more months. In this case I would not have bought.

Keep In Contact With Your Adviser   I will ring my adviser before I make any move to purchase any large object. I need to know whether I should buy it in our personal names or whether I should buy it in the company names. He is well versed in these areas and because of the changing tax laws only he can keep up to all of the new regulations. He will tell me how to buy it and why to buy it in that identity.

When you are setting up a business you must also know whether to set it up in a company or as a partnership. If you don't seek advice first and find that you have to then change it, then this can cost you a lot of wasted money. It is far cheaper to seek advice first. Keep in close contact with your accountant. My accountant is also my adviser. I would talk to him on average about three times a month, minimum. My accountant knows what my financial goals are and he is helping me achieve them. My accountant has attended some of the seminars that I have been to and if he feels it would be beneficial for me to be at a seminar he will ring me and let me know. You must keep the communication up with your accountant.

For tax planning I automatically will contact my accountant on 1 February and again on 1 May each year. Early in May, all of my financial books will be sent to the accountant. They will have all of the up-to-date figures of the financial year so far and also the predictions of income and expenses for the rest of the financial year. This will be for May and up to 30 June. We now have two months to look at our tax planning.

There might be a situation where we have to sell some shares, or contribute more money to superannuation, or to pay interest in advance on some loans. There are many ways to plan your finances before the financial year has finished. Once 30 June has passed, then it is too late. If your accountant does not view your books before 30 June then I would look for another proactive accountant. Your present accountant will be costing you a lot of lost money.

If you feel your adviser is not conservative enough for you and the suggestions of what to do with your money sound too risky, then tell him. You might feel more comfortable in getting a second opinion. Don't invest your money too quickly. Put a small amount of your portfolio into an investment and see how you feel. Your investments are something that you do over your lifetime and not something that must be completed next week. Never be in a hurry. The opportunities will always be there tomorrow. Walk, don't run at first.

What you invest into will depend on your total financial

situation, your personal circumstances and what you are comfortable with yourself. What a friend of yours might be comfortable with you might be very uncomfortable with. This is fine. Go with your gut feeling. If you feel pressured into buying something then back away and come back next week. You need time to think. Use it. You may need to see maybe three financial advisers before you are comfortable with one. Choose carefully. Never be afraid to say that you are a conservative investor.

Your accountant/adviser will not know all of the answers. My adviser will sometimes inform me that he doesn't know how to solve a particular problem, or he does not know the answer to a question. He will sometimes discuss with me that it will be beneficial to seek advice from a specialist in this area. This might mean that we have to employ the services of a tax lawyer who will be able to give us the best advice. As long as we are getting expert advice I am quite happy in paying someone who is more specialised in doing the work we need. Again the money is well spent.

A good solicitor is worth paying for also, as they can also save you a lot of money if they know their job well. You will often call on your solicitor if you need contracts to be drawn up for purchasing and selling property and businesses. Make sure that your solicitor and accountant are willing to work together as a team on some of your future projects that are likely to arise.

PLAYING SNAKES AND LADDERS

When you begin school you have gone to square number one in the game of 'Snakes and Ladders'. Your aim is to win the game by getting to square number 100. Some people will travel forward a lot faster by running up the ladders and bypassing some of the paths to success. Others will go flying backwards down the snakes only to try again. But most of the school years are structured to help you on the correct path. But once you leave school you are really now controlling your own path and you have the choice of which way you go.

As you get into the senior years of secondary school you are asked to choose your subjects that you will concentrate on over the final few years at school. It is important that you have some basic mathematics behind you. I personally did not do business maths or accountancy at school. But the more you understand numbers the more you will understand how the numbers tell a story.

I recommend that you buy every newspaper that has a money section in it. This is usually once a week and it covers all areas of finance. Often there are segments where people have written in to ask questions and answers are given. Many of these questions will be the sort of questions that you want the answers to yourself. Some of the answers you will not understand but it will make you start thinking on that line of questioning.

In many of these articles I do not follow their recommendations because I do not feel it is the best way for me to personally invest. It might be a perfect way for you to invest. This is fine. I read these articles with a very open mind and look deeply at the opinion of some of these writers. Sometimes I disagree with some of the articles but when I read a similar article some time later I see some point of view that will be very beneficial to my investing. You too must read these articles with an open mind and try to see where the writer's opinion is coming from. Always listen to other people's opinions and don't always believe that your way of thinking is the correct way of thinking.

I invest differently now compared to five years ago, and in areas that I said I would never consider. Eleven years ago I did not know what a share was and I was only interested in investing in property. But now, I know how to arm myself with knowledge so that I can continue to build a strong investment portfolio.

13

BUYING OR BUILDING YOUR OWN BUSINESS

Buying or building your own business can be the best way to leverage your time. Mary and I bought a small fast food business in 1985. At that time we had taught in schools for five years and wanted to look at doing something different for a while and could always go back to teaching if we wanted. When we bought this business we did not do a lot of homework and we spoke to the accountant of the vendor of the business, which in hindsight was a mistake. He is likely to have been biased toward his own established client rather than us.

I worked in the business for two months on every weekend for every minute that the business was open. This gave me a good understanding of how the business worked and what sort of demand it would have on me. Before anyone buys a business they must work in the business for every hour that it is open to get the feel of what it is like working for such extended hours. Don't believe that you are going to buy a business that you can be present only when you want to be. At first you will find that you will do many hours of hands-on work and as the years progress you can cut back on the hours until you do not have to be in the business at all. At this stage the business is now working for you. You no longer have to work for the business. Your staff are now running the business. It must now run well without you.

Many people go into business because they no longer want to work for their boss and they feel that they can run their own business very well. Don't be mistaken by thinking that if you are a good employee then automatically you will be very good at running your own business. A person that can make the best bread in town can buy a business and still find that the business goes backwards very quickly.

DON'T BUY YOURSELF A JOB

Many people who buy a business are just buying themselves a job. They have to be working in the business or the business will not survive. Often the business controls them and they have no control over the business. The business tells them when they can have time off and when they can't.

Your business will affect your lifestyle and often control your income. You have to take control of the business and thus control the amount of income that you want to come out of the business. By building the business up you can control what income you want to come out of the business. You can double or triple or even increase your income more than this, if you are willing to put the work into expanding your business.

When you are employed your income is controlled by

your employer. When you own your own business your income is controlled by you. Initially, when you start in your business, you might have to put any money that you make back into the business. Make sure that you don't get caught up into always putting money back into your business unless the profits obviously increase every time you do it. If by injecting more money back into your business you are not increasing your profit, then put this money into other investments. If you put $20,000 into house investments you might find that the return on your money is far better than reinvesting the money back into your business.

Don't rely on your business to be your only investment. Look at other investments as well. While you are self-employed in your own business you are in a risky position. If this is your only form of income then you are in a very high-risk position. An employee can become redundant at any time and a self-employed person can always have opposition opening up against them and will lose part of their market. Don't rely on the business alone to supply you with a comfortable retirement. The cash flow from the business should be directed into investments in property and shares.

KEEP AN EYE ON THE NUMBERS

At the end of every week you must be able to state what your profit has been for the week. The same must be the case for every month and every quarter of the year. If you don't know your profit exactly for every timeframe, then you are asking for trouble. You must be able to work out what percentage your wages are in comparison to your turnover and your profit. You must be able to compare these figures with previous figures and make sure that your overall profit is increasing every year. If your yearly profit is staying the same then I believe that you are going backwards.

If you don't know how to compare figures then you need to buy some books or go to seminars to learn these things. You will always find some profit-improving technique at each of these seminars. Don't forget that a vast majority of businesses fail because the finances aren't monitored closely.

The entity that you buy the business in is also very important. Your accountant will be able to advise you on whether you should own the business as a partnership or whether you should own it within a family trust. The way your business is set up is very important. Especially in the area of tax planning.

EMPLOYING OTHER PEOPLE TO LEVERAGE YOUR OWN TIME

When you own a business you want to leverage your own time by employing other people. To work out whether it is worth putting on another staff member you must look at what the staff member will cost you and what extra profit you will gain by having this new staff member. Again do your maths well.

Let's assume that to employ one more staff member it will cost you a total of $20 an hour. This $20 includes the wage, superannuation, training, workers' compensation insurance and any other staff expense. Therefore you will want your new staff member to bring in at least $25 an hour gross profit for you, so that for each staff member you put on you will increase your own profit by $5 an hour. Therefore if you put on another six staff members your overall profit will need to increase by $30 an hour or more. If you can successfully do this, you will be able to leverage your own time.

Our small business started off with four staff members and we built it up to about 20 staff members in seven years. The more staff members you have and the more profit you make the more you are leveraging both your time and your money. The more money you make, the more you can put into other investments.

FINANCING YOUR BUSINESS

If you have enough equity in your house you can use this equity to buy a business. Obviously, this depends on both the cost of the business and the amount of equity that you have in your house. Any interest on a loan for the purchase of a business is fully tax deductible, so if you have extra money being produced by your business don't use it to pay off your business loan until your house has been paid out fully. You don't even have to pay out your house as I discussed in previous chapters. You might use the extra cash flow to fund the purchase of other investments. Only do this when you are comfortable that you can service all loans. If you are uneasy about all of your loans then pay off your house more until the time that you become comfortable.

When buying a business it is very hard to gauge how the business will go so you might want to pay off your house for at least the first year. By this time you will have a good idea of the cash flow produced from the business. Then you can start investing.

Is this what we did? No, this is not. Due to the lack of financial knowledge at the time, we paid off a high percentage of the business loan. Then I found out that the business loan was fully tax deductible so we then started to buy investment properties. Once we saw the reliable cash flow from the business and knew how we could increase profits of the business by introducing a few strategies, we should have started to invest. At this time there was no need to pay any more off the business as the taxman was helping us with our loan expenses.

If you need to buy a large piece of equipment that might cost you say $20,000, then you should commercially lease it so that you do not tie up the $20,000. This $20,000 is enough to put down as a deposit for a new investment house or to use to buy say $40,000 worth of quality shares. Your accountant will set up your leasing arrangements so that it is most favourable to your investment strategies.

A Common Mistake Many people sell their houses and buy a business with the money. Say, you have $150,000 from the house and you use it to buy a business outright. You have no loan on the business at all. You then decide to buy a new house to live in and because you have no money left in the bank you have to borrow the lot. The interest that you pay on this house loan is not tax deductible. You should have obtained a loan of $150,000 for your business and used the $150,000 that you had in the bank as security for this loan. Your loan would have been fully tax deductible. You then buy your new house for $150,000 using the money in the bank and the security for your business loan is now transferred across to your private home.

In other words, the bank now is holding a mortgage over your private home as security for your $150,000 loan on the business. The purpose of the loan determines whether it will be tax deductible. In this situation the purpose of the loan was to buy the business and that is why it is tax deductible. It does not matter what security is being held for the loan. The security being held can be either personal or business. It makes no difference.

Let us look at what you save by setting up your loan this way:

$$\$150,000 \times 8.5\% = \$12,750 \text{ interest per year.}$$

If you are on the top tax bracket your tax refund will be:

$$\$12,750 \times 47\% = \$5993 \text{ tax refund.}$$

Therefore it will cost you $5993 cash flow less per year if you have the loan for your business and not for your private home. Over a 10-year term this would save you:

$$\$5993 \times 10 \text{ years} = \$59,930.$$

This would have allowed you to put two deposits on two investment properties during those 10 years, which would now have increased with capital growth. Can you see how your planning on your loans is so important?

BUSINESS SYSTEMS

To develop a business you must develop a system that will run entirely by itself. You cannot rely on one staff member because if he is away you have no one else to replace him. Your business must be an organisation that is built up with systems and the staff work within these systems. Any one staff member must be able to be replaced by many other staff members. The system must run without you being there. To develop these systems will require a lot of trial and error. You will always be able to change these systems for the better.

If you don't develop these systems then the business will rely too much on you. Often you will find businesses that are doing extremely well but the owner cannot step outside the business. The owner finds himself working more and more hours every week and their family life and recreation life suffers tremendously.

You must have fun in your life. If you haven't the time to relax the way you want to then you are doing something wrong. To work harder will not solve this problem but make it worse. I once read, 'If you can't do your job in forty hours then you are doing something wrong'. Don't forget what financial freedom means. You must have the money but you must also have the free time to enjoy it. You must work smart.

Realise that going into business is not going to be easy at first. The rewards come later on as your business develops. There are a large percentage of first-time businesses that do not last for more than a few years. You again must do your own homework and do it well. Like buying houses, don't buy for emotional reasons. You must only look at business reasons and investment reasons for you to go ahead with the purchase of a business. You must realise that your business is your life. Find a way that you can own it but still be free of it.

If you have a problem with the business then the problem is not usually the business itself. The problem may be you. Until you can change the way you see your business you will keep on having the same problems. You must see your business as a saleable item that is generating a good cash flow for you or for the people that will buy it next.

CAN YOU GET THINGS DONE?

For you to contemplate going into your own business you must be the sort of person who gets things done. You must be able to get results. When you are an employee you know that you will be paid at the end of the week even if you don't succeed in getting everything done. This is not the case when you are in business. You must get things done today and if you can't do it then you must delegate to others to get things done today.

This will require leadership skills. If at present you feel that you have not got leadership skills then that is fine. Just go out and get them. You can always become a leader. There are so many excellent books and tapes that you can buy that will really help you on improving your leadership skills.

You must be a person who acts upon your ideas. Excellent ideas are not enough if you cannot act upon them immediately. You must be a doer and if you are not, then you must become one. A doer will find ways to follow through on problems. A non-doer will find reasons why he should not follow through. The idea of getting things done or to simplify work procedures is of value only when it is acted upon. You must act upon your ideas. Unless you do something with your ideas you gain nothing.

I often hear people say that if they went into business 10 years ago then they would be far better off. Or that they think the town could do with a good bookshop and that it would be a very profitable business, but they themselves do nothing about it. A good idea acted upon brings enormous mental satisfaction.

The other thing that will determine your success in business will not necessarily be your brains or your business plan. It will be persistence, persistence and more persistence. We were asked by friends why we would go into a fast food shop when we were both doing well in teaching. It was as if people thought that we were taking a step backwards. I loved our business. Yes it was a hard challenge but one that anyone could achieve if they really put their mind to it.

This does not mean that you must go into business to become financially free. That is not the case at all. There are many people out there who are on below average incomes that have enormous property and share portfolios. Mary and I would still have achieved financial freedom if we did not go into business for ourselves. It is not the money that you make, it is what you do with it. What other people see as limitations, you must see as possibilities.

14

SHARES – AN INTRODUCTION

I remember our financial adviser telling us that we owned too many houses and not enough shares. Actually we had no shares at all. He wanted us to buy just a small amount of shares so we would experience what it was like to own shares. So, we bought $5000 worth of shares. This was the beginning. We watched these shares in the newspaper and learned about dividends and price earning ratios and a lot of other terms that we did not know anything about beforehand. This was the best way to learn. As soon as you put money into anything you learn a little bit more about it.

The next shares we bought were known as 'blue chip' shares. Today we still own those shares and over the years they have performed very well. Over the long term the original shares have given excellent capital growth and the income from the dividends has also provided a good cash flow. Over the past 10 years we have added more money to our share portfolio and with the money we receive in dividends we usually reinvest it back into buying more shares. Also we have had the capital growth of the whole share portfolio over the time that we have had them.

Shares are a different kind of investment compared to property. You can sell your shares today for the price that they are listed at for today. You will have trouble selling your house immediately like that and you will not know what price you will get until someone has offered a price, which you accept. You can sell a small parcel of shares. You do not have to sell them all at once. You can't sell just part of your house. You must sell your entire house.

Don't believe that the shares are more risky than property. They are only very risky when you do not know what you are doing. Just like property you must do your homework or have someone else do your homework for you before you buy the shares. You can manage your risk by buying shares that suit your risk.

I do not trade shares in the short term as to me there is more risk. I have not learned enough yet to do short-term trading. I have tried trading in the futures market, but I was not successful at this and for the moment I've put this sort of high-risk trading on hold until I learn a lot more about it. If you begin to trade the Futures then you must only do it with money that you are able to lose. Over 85 per cent of traders of the Futures Market lose money. I was one of them.

If you are a conservative investor and practise the strategy of 'buy and hold', good. The capital gain on shares would be at about the same percentage as property. It depends on what book or newspaper you read. Some will say that shares out-perform property while others might state that property out-performs shares. To accelerate your return on your money you can borrow money to buy shares. Usually you will borrow through the lending arm of your broker. This borrowing is called 'margin lending'. If this margin lending is done correctly and conservatively then you can manage the risk level that you want to take.

When I invest in shares I look at the long-term investment. I do not look at putting money into shares to make a quick profit and to sell in six months time so I can spend the profit elsewhere. This is not my strategy at all. I have always seen the purchase of the shares to be with money that I do not plan to use for many years to come. Just like property, I want the capital growth to be reasonable and any income from rents or dividends I will use to buy more property or more shares. I see the share market as another vehicle to help people achieve financial freedom. It is something that you should study and become very comfortable with. Don't forget that the more you learn about the share market the less risky it is. It is just like property.

THE SHARE MARKET CAN BE VOLATILE

It is common for share prices to drop quickly and to increase quickly. This does not mean that the company is worth less or more. It's just that the public believes that the price will go up so there are more buyers than sellers, which pushes the market up. When the majority of people believe that the share price is over-valued and will go down, they will sell and there will be more sellers than buyers. This will obviously push the share price down.

Often the share price is determined by the fear or greed of people and not by the value of the company.

If you are to invest in shares for the long term then this volatility should not concern you. You might find that your shares have decreased in value some months after you bought them but this is fine because over the long term they will have increased in value if you have bought strong conservative shares.

When you buy shares make sure that you are getting reasonable value for your money. The market value of the shares that you are about to buy might be too high for what the fundamentals of the company show it should be worth. Because the share price fluctuates up and down make sure you wait for the price of the shares to fall to a fair value before you decide to buy in. If you hold shares that you feel are way over-valued then you would consider selling them and obtain an excellent profit, as they are likely to fall in price in the future. When they do fall in price, and if you still believe that they are an excellent share then you can buy back in, at a far more reasonable price.

THE STOCKBROKER

I use a stockbroker and I pay an extra premium because I get full advice as well. You can use brokers who are discount brokers who will not give you advice but will only execute your buy and sell orders as quickly as possible. I will nearly always discuss a purchase with my financial adviser before the order is given to the stockbroker. Usually my financial adviser has already discussed opportunities with my broker and then rings me to discuss whether I want to buy or sell.

Because I don't follow my shares closely enough myself, I find it very comforting to know that my adviser and my broker are knowledgeable in what is going on with the shares that I own or I'm thinking about owning.

By having a full service broker I am also able to be allocated good company shares that are about to list on the stock exchange. To be able to buy these shares when the general public can't until they are listed on the board at the exchange, has made a lot of money for me. Often when they begin trading these shares have already increased dramatically in value in comparison to what I have paid for the initial allocation. If the share fundamentals do not look positive in the long term then I will sell immediately and take a good profit. This profit has always far outweighed what it costs me for a full service broker.

If you were to trade often then it would be more advantageous to agree on a reasonable brokerage rate for trading. A full service broker will cost you about 2 per cent of the transaction. Usually with a discount trader they will charge you a flat fee per transaction. When you begin in shares it might be worth having a full service broker at first as you will need guidance. Later on you might believe that you can do it better yourself and thus use a discount broker.

Over time you will learn more about the share market and the shares that you wish to buy or have already bought. As you gain this extra knowledge about shares you will be able to put your own opinion forward when your broker is suggesting to buy or sell a particular share. Don't forget that the final decision is yours. If you are not comfortable in buying a share then all you have to say is, 'No'.

DIVIDENDS

When a company makes a profit it will usually pay the shareowners a dividend out of these profits. With the rest of the profits they will usually reinvest back into the company to pay off some debt or to expand the company.

I have always bought shares that are paying franked dividends. This means that the company that is paying the dividend has already paid company tax on the dividend, which has been 36 per cent in the past up to 1 July 2000. This has now become 34 per cent. Therefore if a franked dividend is paid to you then you will receive a tax credit for the tax that has already been paid by the company. This tax credit will lessen the tax that you have to pay on your income. The tax credits that you obtain with your dividends are also known as Imputation Credits.

Because of the imputation credits, it is advantageous to buy the shares that are paying fully franked dividends in the name of the lowest taxpayer in your partnership. This is because they will still pay the lower marginal tax on the dividend but will receive the full 34 per cent tax credit to offset against their other tax. Also when you own your own private superannuation fund the imputation credits that you obtain on shares that you can buy in this fund are of great benefit. Your superannuation fund is only taxed at 15 per cent but you will receive a 34 per cent credit for your imputation credits. You can organise your contribution to your superannuation fund and the use of buying shares within this fund in a way that you can run your superannuation fund without paying any tax at all. I will expand on this more in the Chapter 15.

FINDING GOOD SHARES

When deciding on what shares to buy there are many factors that you can consider that will determine whether you should buy or not. Unfortunately if you considered all factors you would never buy as they would never all meet the criteria that you are looking for.

You must consider the history of the company over the last three years and the forecast of what it will achieve in the next two years. Not that the future is at all totally predictable. You are looking for a company that is growing in size, in turnover and in profit. You are looking for a company that can create a good return on the money that it is reinvesting back into the company itself.

It is important to look at the management of the company and know what sort of previous history this manager has had with this company and maybe with his previous companies. The manager must act as if he is the owner of the company. See if the manager also has a large holding of shares in their own company. If they have, then you know that they are going to work hard for the company so that the share price lifts and thus they make more money themselves. Also look at the product that the company is producing and introducing. Is the demand for this product increasing?

Don't try to hold too many stocks at once. When you first start you might only buy two stocks and as your portfolio grows you might own up to 10 stocks. But don't forget that you want to start looking after and understanding your own portfolio, so if you have more than 10 stocks then you are finding more work for yourself. If I had invested $100,000 into shares then I would own about five different stocks for that size portfolio.

It is worth you buying the book called, *The Warren Buffett Way*, by Robert Hagstrom Jr. Warren discusses what he looks for before he buys any shares. He definitely does his homework to the extreme but then he is one of the most successful investors in the world. Warren doesn't speculate about the direction of the market. Which way the market goes over the short term does not concern him. He knows that if he has bought correctly then over time the true value of the share will be shown by the market price.

The speculator tries to buy and sell, depending on whether he thinks the price is about to rise or fall. The true investor only buys good shares at what he considers are reasonable prices.

MARGIN LENDING

Just as you can borrow money to buy property you can borrow money to buy shares. You can use the equity in your home to obtain a line of credit and thus buy shares with this. You can also use the shares that you own and the shares that you are going to buy to be security for the loan that you have on the shares.

The broker that you are buying your shares through will be willing to lend you more money to buy more shares when your portfolio is worth $20,000 or more.

The amount your broker will lend you on your shares will depend on how secure your broker believes that your shares are.

Let's assume that you hold $20,000 worth of blue chip

shares. The broker will lend you up to 70 per cent of the value of the shares.

Therefore he will lend you 70 per cent × $20,000 = $14,000, which you can now use to buy more shares. Again as your share portfolio increases the margin lender will increase the possible loan amount.

Assume that you have $30,000 to invest in shares. You can buy up to $100,000 worth of shares using your $30,000 cash and the lending arm will hold your shares as security for their $70,000 that you borrow.

$30,000	Your money
$70,000	Loan amount
$100,000	Shares purchased

In this case you have borrowed 70 per cent of the value of your share portfolio. Usually 70 per cent is the most you can borrow using your shares as security. For me this is far too high. If your portfolio value fell to say $90,000 then your gearing has become $70,000 ÷ $90,000 = 78%, and the lending organisation would send you a margin call.

A margin call relates to the action of the broker's lending arm ringing you and requesting that you deposit money into your share loan account, known as your margin lending account.

You have 24 hours to deposit this money or the broker has the right to sell some of your shares so that the loan/value ratio of your account decreases below the maximum lending percentage.

This will occur usually when your loan/value ratio is close to the 70 per cent maximum and the share price falls so now the market value of your shares has decreased, but your loan amount is still the same. Therefore your loan/value ratio has risen above 70 per cent which is higher than allowed.

Instead of depositing money into your loan account to make your loan/value ratio decrease, you are also allowed to provide more shares to the lending arm. These shares can be used for more security.

You would have to bring your borrowings back to 70 per cent, so on a $90,000 portfolio you would only be able to borrow $90,000 × 70% = $63,000. Because your loan is $70,000 you would have to find the money to pay off the $70,000 – $63,000 = $7000 immediately. If you can't pay off the $7000 immediately then the lending arm has the right to sell some of your shares, now at a lower price, so that you fall under the 70 per cent gearing again. You will have already made a recorded loss on your shares.

I will never leverage myself over 50 per cent in shares and a more comfortable amount for me is less than 40 per cent. If I do leverage at the 50 per cent level then I will also have access to other money that I can use if I ever receive a margin call. To this day I have never received a margin call.

When you obtain a loan to buy your shares the interest on the loan is tax deductible just as if the loan was for property. You can also pay your interest on your margin lending annually in advance and thus claim for this full interest amount as a tax deduction in the year that it is paid. You would usually do this just before 30 June, the end of the financial year. So if you have a margin loan of say $100,000 and you are in a position where you are in the highest tax bracket then you would consider the advantages of paying interest in advance on the loan.

Assume your interest rate on the margin loan is 8.5 per cent.

$$\$100,000 \times 8.5\% = \$8500$$

By paying this $8500 annually in advance before 30 June you can claim the full $8500 as a tax deduction in that tax year. Your tax rate would be 47 per cent as you are in the top tax bracket, so your saving would be:

$$\$8500 \times 47\% = \$3995$$

DOLLAR COST AVERAGING

Let's assume that you have $5000 to invest into shares so you decide to buy bank shares. The buying price is $25.00 so you are able to buy 200 shares. 200 shares × $25.00 = $5000. All of the fundamentals of the bank look like a very strong company with great opportunity to increase in value over time. Naturally, always in buying shares you are assuming (hoping) that the price will rise. But the price goes against you and it drops to $22.00. You now feel that the share is very cheap so you decide to buy another $5000 worth of shares at $22.00, 227 shares × $22.00 = $4994. Again the market goes against you and the price of the shares drops to $20.00, and again you buy another $5000 worth of shares at the $20.00 price, 250 shares × $20.00 = $5000. So what is your average price of your shares?

$$200 \text{ at } \$25.00 = \$5000$$
$$227 \text{ at } \$22.00 = \$4994$$
$$\underline{250} \text{ at } \underline{\$20.00} = \underline{\$5000}$$
$$\text{Total } \underline{677} \text{ shares } \underline{\$14,994}$$

$$\$14,994 \div 677 \text{ shares} = \$22.15.$$

You now know that if you sell your total shares for above $22.15 then you will make a profit. If the shares return to the higher price of $25.00 then you have made $2.85 per share profit, which will be a total of $1901 for the 677 shares.

So if the share price is falling then you can see that it is a good theory to buy as the shares cost less and less. BUT THIS THEORY IS NOT ALWAYS SO GOOD IN PRACTICE. As the shares decrease in price to $22.00 you are becoming defensive (fear) and worried about the money that you have lost. In this case you might buy another $5000 worth hoping that they will now go up. But what happens? The shares continue to go down in price and you are now losing more money. When the shares get to $20.00 your mind is playing tug-of-war with itself:

1. If I put more money into buying more shares at $20.00 the benefits of dollar averaging is there, but
2. If I put more money into buying more shares at $20.00 the market will keep on going down so therefore I am just wasting more money.

What do you do? Buy more shares at $20.00 at this stage? Don't forget that so far you have bought

$$200 \times \$25.00 = \$5000$$
$$227 \times \$22.00 = \underline{\$4994}$$
$$\underline{\$9994}$$

At present these shares have dropped to $427 \times \$20.00 =$ $\$8540$. You have already lost $\$9994 - \$8540 = \$1454$ of your money, which is 14.5 per cent of your investment. Aren't you meant to make money out of investing and not lose it?

Initially, you will find dollar averaging a very hard concept to follow, but as you invest more in shares over time you will find that you will buy shares because you believe that they are cheap. You will consider their present price more important than considering what price you bought the other shares for. I remember buying bank shares for $\$7.50$, but when the price dropped to about $\$5.50$ I bought as many as I could afford. A large percentage of the money which I used to buy the lower priced shares was borrowed money. The return I made on this purchase over the years was:

> Money invested $\$20,000$ own money
> $\underline{\$40,000}$ borrowed funds
> $\underline{\$60,000}$ Total purchase
>
> $\$60,000 \div \$5.50$ a share = 10,909 shares.
> Today's price about $\$25.90$
> 10,909 shares $\times \$25.90$ each = $\$282,543$.

So my initial investment of my own money of $\$20,000$ has now increased by $\$222,543$. $\$282,543 - \$40,000$ (initial borrowings) $- \$20,000$ (my money) = $\$222,543$, which is 1113 per cent return over a nine-and-a-half-year term. This is a bit better than 5 per cent return per year I'd have received if I had my money in the bank. Also in the beginning, the interest on the $40,000 loan would have nearly been covered by the dividend. But with a dividend yield now at 4.5 per cent – ($282,543 × 4.5% yield now = $12,714 dividend a year). This still doesn't take into consideration the advantages of the imputation credits that come with the dividend.

It begs the question: Where will you park your spare money – in the bank or will you buy part of the bank by buying shares?

DIVIDEND YIELDS OF FULLY FRANKED SHARES

Let us assume that the dividend on a share is $1.15 a year and that the share price is $25.90. The dividend yield that will be stated in the newspaper will be:

$$\frac{1.15}{25.9} \times 100 = 4.4\%$$

This is not your true return if you are comparing it to the interest you will get if you have your money in the bank. To obtain this true return comparison you must take into consideration your imputation credits as well. Based on the company paying 34 cents tax on the full dividend before it is allocated to you, your imputation credit is:

$$\text{Imputation Credit} = 1.15 \times \frac{34}{66} = .59$$

Therefore the grossed up dividend is equal to the dividend $1.15 + the imputation credit .59 cents ($1.15 + .59 = $1.74).

To see the true value of the yield:

$$\frac{\$1.74}{25.90} \times 100 = 6.7\% \text{ True Yield}$$

Now compare this to a deposit in the bank.

Note, the company tax rate fell to 34 per cent on 1 July 2000 and will fall to 30 per cent on 1 July 2001. This will mean that the imputation credits will fall also.

TAKING A LOSS

Say, you have bought 1000 shares in a company for $5.00 each, as you heard that they have an excellent chance of striking oil tomorrow. Six months later they are worth $3.50 and another six months later on they are worth $1.50. You are worried as your investment of $5000 (1000 × $5.00) is now worth only $1500 (1000 × $1.50). So you are down $3500 on your $5000 investment. You have lost 70 per cent ($3500/ $5000) of your initial investment. You wonder what to do.

Check with your broker to see where the shares are likely to go from today. Do not even think about what price you paid for them. Your purchase price is irrelevant. You must decide what you are going to do with the shares only on what you predict will happen in the future. If there is little chance of the shares improving in price then take a loss and put your money into a share that has a far more positive outlook. You must monitor your share portfolio and if there are any duds that have not got a positive future, sell them and look for something better. The capital loss that you incur can be applied against any capital gain that you have achieved, so you will not have to suffer the full loss.

Look at it a different way. Let's assume that you have bought 1000 shares for $5.00 each. Over the next two years these shares have risen to $10.00 each so now they are worth $10,000. You believe that at the price of $10.00 these shares are very over-priced and that the price will fall over the next year. You decide to sell the 1000 shares and you have a capital gain of $5000 that will be taxed as capital gains. You also own some blue chip shares that have fallen in value but are still very good shares to keep. You have worked out that if you sell these shares now you will realise a $5000 capital loss, which will match your capital gain, so now you will have no capital gain to be taxed at all. You have saved the amount of the would-be tax. You can then look around for some better buys.

PLAY WITH THE NUMBERS

The return on your investment in shares can be very huge if you leverage it correctly. In this exercise I will show you how to use equity in your own home that is just sitting there and not being used, and show you how you can obtain a substantial return on your money.

Many people have $40,000 of equity in their own homes that they are not aware of that they can use to invest. Some people will never see the opportunities to invest this money. You must take this money and use it to invest or otherwise you are missing lost opportunities.

Assumptions: $40,000 available funds from the equity in your home.

Interest rate is 8.5% Fixed, Interest only
Dividend Yield = 4% Fully Franked at 34%
Marginal Tax rate you are on = 30%

You organise a $40,000 loan using your own property as security. You buy $80,000 worth of good quality shares using another $40,000 of margin lending. The margin lender will hold the title of the $80,000 worth of shares as security for the $40,000 loan that it gives you.

Home equity funds	$40,000
Margin Lending	$40,000
Shares Purchased	$80,000

The interest on both loans is 8.5 per cent. ($80,000 × 8.5% = $6800 a year.)

4% dividend = $80,000 × 4% = $3200 Dividend
Imputation Credit = $3200 × 0.34/0.66 = $1648.
Grossed Up Dividend = $3200 + $1648 = $4848.

When you are calculating your dividend income for taxation purposes you must add both the dividend and the franking credit together.

Taxable income = Dividend Grossed Up	$4848
Minus Interest Expenses	$6800
Total Taxable Loss	−$1952
Tax refund on $1952 = $1952 × 30% = $586	

The cash flow situation would be:

| Dividend | +$3200 |
| Interest | −$6800 |

Tax refund	+$ 586
Tax Credit	+$1,648
Loss per year	−$1366

Over the next five years, don't forget, the dividend will usually keep on increasing as well. So your total cost per year to service both loans, is $1366. ($1366 ÷ 52 weeks = $26.27 a week.)

Over the next five years let us look at what happens to the value of our shares. The cost to service this loan over the five years will be $1366 × 5 = $6830. Assume just 8 per cent capital growth on your shares per year for five years.

To calculate then compounding capital growth on your shares for the five years at 8 per cent per year remember that you just multiply each year by 1.08.

$$\$80,000 \times 1.08\% =$$
1. $86,400
2. $93,312
3. $100,777
4. $108,839
5. $117,546

Capital growth over the five years equals:

$117,546	Value of shares
−$80,000	Initial Loans
$37,546	Capital Growth

To find out what return you have made on your money of $6830 that it has cost you in cash flow, you must also subtract this from the gain. You have turned $6830 cash flow into $37,546 – capital growth.

$$\$37,546$$
$$-\$6830$$
$$\$30,716$$

Therefore our return on our out of pocket money will be $30,716 ÷ $6830 = 450% return on your money for the five years.

Again, why would you leave your money in the bank? Have you any equity in your house that you could be using to buy more shares? As the capital growth increases over the years you would again borrow more using your growing equity. In a very short time you would find that you would not have to put any of your own money in at all to service the loans. The dividends would service the loans completely. Look at it this way. You are now making money out of nothing.

15

DO-IT-YOURSELF
SUPERANNUATION

To many people superannuation is seen as a form of saving. I see it as a form of investing. The government sees it as a form of saving for future years when there may not be enough money available to pay for all of the pensions. So if you save money yourself then hopefully you won't require the pension.

As you know, employee superannuation is a compulsory payment of part of your wage into an allocated superannuation fund. At present it is 8 per cent, and it will increase to 9 per cent in July 2002.

If you think that this money, placed with a superannuation fund, will give you a luxury lifestyle once you have retired then think again. The present annual income you are on will be a lot more than what your superannuation will give you once you retire. Your superannuation income will be determined by how early you start contributing and how much you contribute over your working life.

The compulsory super contribution might be adequate

for some people but their lifestyle will have to be fairly simple. Let's assume that your only assets when you retire are your house and your superannuation which is worth about $300,000. If you were going to live for another 20 years then your retirement income would be close to $25,000 a year. Not much! Forget about that overseas holiday you wanted or the new car you promised yourself!

If you are male you are likely to live to the age of about 80. Females on average will live a little longer. What if you live longer? At what age can you retire?

You will have no control over your life if you only have compulsory superannuation – your money will determine when you will be able to retire. Don't allow this to happen. When your super runs out you will have to live on the pension. Can you live 'comfortably' on about $8000 a year? Money is now controlling your life or rather lack of it. You must turn this situation around. You must control the money.

I read in the newspaper of a young man in his 20s who ideally would like to live off a combination of part-time work and investments by the age of 50. This is limiting himself. He could have a life of freedom by the time he is in his 30s if he knew how to do it and had the desire to do it. If he found this a bit difficult then he could aim for his 40s. There is no rule that you have to reach a certain age before you can retire. We set those rules ourselves. We set our own limitations.

If you are new at investing and you own your own home but no investment property or shares, then extra superannuation contributions are probably not for you. You will have to have the guaranteed percentage of 8 per cent put into superannuation and this will come out of your employer's pocket and not yours.

What I would do. My first goal would be to pay as much as I could off the housing loan until I was comfortable enough to start investing. I would then invest in property and use negative gearing to keep my taxable income down as far as possible and buy more property or begin investing in shares, slowly introducing margin lending so I could buy more shares. All of the money I produce from this I know I have access to at any time by selling the asset that I want to, if I want to.

WHEN DID WE START CONTRIBUTING TO SUPER?

While we were teaching I could contribute 2.5 per cent of my wage to super and my employer contributed 2.5 per cent as well. When I bought the shop I cashed in my superannuation as I needed every dollar I could find. Mary remained teaching so her superannuation continued as previously.

When we both became self-employed we each contributed $3000 a year to our superannuation fund. This $3000 was at the time the maximum a self-employed person could contribute while having the full amount tax deductible. During this time we were introduced to the concept of term insurance which is just like insuring a house except we were insuring our own lives. Both Mary and I had this insurance. We would pay a premium at the beginning of the year and would have to repay this premium each year on that anniversary. Buying insurance through our superannuation fund was cheaper than if we bought it in our personal names. It is also tax effective to buy the insurance cover within our superannuation.

You should have enough insurance cover so that if one of you dies all of your debts will be covered. It is also very important that both husband and wife are insured. Many couples only have insurance on the husband.

In about 1992, we created our own private superannuation fund. There are many tax benefits to be gained by managing your own superannuation fund. One of these advantages is that you can manage a separate share portfolio within your superannuation fund.

You will find that you will only pay 15 per cent tax on the income that is derived and shares that are bought after 1 October 1999 will only be subjected to a capital gains tax of 10 per cent. Because of these tax advantages the portfolio will grow faster than if it was invested in your own name.

Do-it-yourself superannuation does not mean that you have to do all of the buying and selling yourself. You can rely on your accountant or broker to help you set up your own superannuation fund and to give you advice on the best investment strategies to take.

Because the costs involved in beginning a private superannuation fund and to maintain it are quite expensive, the benefits of the fund were not obvious until two years later as the amount of assets within the fund increased. Each year in June, once we worked out our financial position for the year, we could use the superannuation fund to help with our tax planning. At that time both Mary and I were able to contribute about $9000 each into the superannuation fund. This money was then fully tax deductible. Therefore with Mary and I both being on the 43 per cent tax bracket at that time we could save 43 per cent of the amount that we contributed, on tax.

Mary	$9000
Sean	$9000
	$18,000 × 43% = $7740

We saved $7740 in tax by contributing the $18,000. But the money that is contributed to the super fund is taxed at 15 per cent so there is superannuation tax of $2700 ($18,000 × 15%). By contributing to the super fund we are $5040 ($7740 − $2700) better off.

By purchasing shares within a super fund you can make sure that you don't pay any tax at all within the super fund. Assume that after three years you have $60,000 worth of shares in the super fund. The dividends on these shares are fully franked and are paying 4.5 per cent.

$$\$60,000 \times 4.5\% = \$2700$$

Imputation credits equal:

$$\$2700 \times 0.34 \div 0.66 = \$1391$$

The grossed-up dividend equals:

$2700	Dividend
+ $1391	Imputation Credit
$4091	

The income in the superannuation fund is taxed at 15 per cent so the tax equals $613 ($4091 × 15%). But we have a tax credit of $1391 so therefore we have more tax credits than we have tax.

$$\$1391 - \$613 = \$778 \text{ in excess credits.}$$

Up to 1 July 2000 any tax credits not used in the same financial year were wasted. You could not transfer them to the next year. You had to use them in the same financial year. I will now show you how to use all of the tax credits.

We have $778 in excess credits which we want to use. (This planning is done in June and must be completed by 30 June each year.) We know that if we contribute money to the super fund then the fund must pay tax on the contribution at the rate of 15 per cent. Therefore, to cancel out our excess credits of $778 we must contribute $5187 ($778 ÷ 15%). Therefore if we want to turn this around the other way, a contribution of $5187 will tax us $778 ($5187 × 15%). If we subtract the excess credits of $778, then we pay zero tax.

But, it gets better than this. Assume we are in the 42 per cent tax bracket then our personal tax savings will be $2179 ($5187 × 42%). We have no tax to pay in our super fund and we have a personal tax savings of $2179. We also own a large share portfolio where the capital gains are taxed at only 15 per cent. This has since changed to 10 per cent, which came into effect on assets, bought after 1 October 1999. To summarise our super fund tax:

Super fund shares	$60,000 × 4.5 dividend	= $2700
Imputation Credits	$2700 × 0.34 ÷ 0.66	= $1391
Contribution to fund		= $5187
	Total	$9278

Tax on $9278 × 15% = $1391
Subtract tax credits = $1391
0 Tax to pay.

On 1 July 2000 the rule concerning the imputation credits changed. Any credits not used in a financial year will now be fully refunded. Therefore you do not have to make sure that all credits will be used up. The aim of the super fund is to minimise tax liabilities and maximise growth within the fund. Now you can see why you must do your tax planning well before 30 June.

Don't be surprised if some of my mathematics or understanding of the above strategy is not correct. This may be the case. That is why I employ an accountant, as it is his job to make sure that all procedures are carried out correctly. He will have a full understanding of all the different changes that they have made over the years, especially in the area of superannuation.

You Cannot Leverage Your Superannuation Fund My superannuation fund does not own any properties at all. It only owns shares and some deposits in a superannuation bank account. The reason why it does not own property is because it cannot borrow money. For the fund to be able to buy property it would have to have the full amount of the purchase price of the house. Also you cannot use margin lending within your superannuation fund so there is no leveraging available within the fund at all.

HOW SUPERANNUATION FUNDS OPERATE

Most people will rely on the compulsory superannuation deposit their employer is putting in for them. As they get to the age of about 30 they see that their investing is non-existent and make the big decision that they had better start doing something about it. They decide to put $3000 a year into super but do nothing else about accumulating investments. What are they thinking? Do they believe that this $3000 a year will give them a comfortable standard of living when they retire? Have they convinced themselves that they do not have to invest in anything else? When asked about their retirement plans their response is, 'I'll be fine because I'm putting extra into super'.

Unfortunately these people are in a bad position because they are ignorant of the reality of the situation. They perceive that they are going to be just fine. They have no other knowledge. Let's work out exactly where someone will be after following this example.

By the age of 40 our subject will have accumulated about $44,000. He continues to add $3000 a year and his return on his fund is about 8 per cent. By the time he retires he has about $295,000 in his super fund. If his return on his assets remains at 8 per cent then he will receive a gross annual income in retirement of about $25,000. Could you live your present lifestyle on $25,000 a year? Let's look at two scenarios of how he will live on his superfund in retirement.

Scenario A   He believes that by the time he dies he wants to have spent nearly all of his money. He has no dependants at all that he wants to leave money to. So he 'believes' that if he spends $35,000 a year then the money will still out-last him. What percentage of his assets is he spending?

$$\frac{\$35,000}{\$295,000} = 11.8\%$$

If his fund is still producing an income of 8 per cent then how long will it be until his money runs out? His money will last about 15 years. What happens if he lives for 20 years?

Scenario B   He decides that he is not going to budget and he is really going to live-it-up once he retires. He is going to spend $1000 a week on himself.

$$\$1000 \text{ per week} \times 52 \text{ weeks} = \$52,000 \text{ a year.}$$

This is 17.6 per cent ($52,000 ÷ $295,000) of his super-fund. Assuming he still earns 8 per cent on his fund, his money will last him only eight years. He will then need to live off the pension. This means that he will go from a spending habit of $52,000 a year to a spending control of $8000 a year, which is 15 per cent (8000 ÷ 52,000) of his previous income.

Is this scary to you? Hopefully it is, as I am not here to hold your hand. If it means that I have to shock you into taking action, well then that's fine by me.

Your ideal situation is that you spend maybe 10 per cent of your total asset value and at the same time your total asset value has a net rate of return of 10 per cent or more.

This will mean that you will never run out of money. So work out how much money you will need.

Assume that you want to retire with a possible spending budget of $2000 a week or $104,000 a year. If you can receive a net rate of return on your net assets of 6 per cent a year then you only want to be spending 6 per cent of your total net assets. How much will you need in net assets?

$$\$104,000 \div 6\% = \$104,000 \times 100/6 = \$1,733,333.$$

Read this number again and remember it.

If you own this amount in net assets and you receive a 6 per cent net return on these net assets and you want to budget on spending $104,000 a year then you can retire from active work today.

Graph 15.1 will help you work out how long your money will last you when you retire.

How does this graph work? You have worked out what percentage of your fund you will live on and you know what rate of return you are receiving on your assets.

Assumptions:	Total assets $500,000
	Return on assets 6%
	Spending per year $35,000
Calculations:	$35,000 ÷ 500,000 = 7%

You find the 7 per cent spending percentage on the left-hand side of your graph. Find the 6 per cent return on the top of your graph. Join these two percentages and you find the number of years until your money runs out. You have enough for 33 years.

Graph 15.1

EXPECTED RATE OF RETURN

Spending % of fund	5%	6%	7%	8%	9%	10%	11%	12%	13%	14%	15%
6%	37										
7%	25	33									
8%	20	23	30								
9%	16	18	22	29							
10%	14	15	17	20	27						
11%	12	14	15	17	20	25					
12%	11	12	13	14	16	19	24				
13%	10	11	11	12	14	15	18	23			
14%	9	10	10	11	12	13	15	17	22		
15%	8	9	9	10	11	12	13	14	16	21	
16%	8	8	9	9	10	10	11	12	14	16	20
17%	7	7	8	8	9	9	10	11	12	13	15
18%	7	7	7	8	8	9	9	10	10	11	13
19%	6	7	7	7	7	8	8	9	9	10	11
20%	6	6	6	7	7	7	8	8	9	9	10

Years to exhaust fund

Calculate your own spending percentage of your funds and your percentage of return on your funds. How long will your money last? Don't forget that you could live until you are 80 years old or even more. Have you enough?

CAN YOU MANAGE YOUR OWN FUND?

Don't expect that you will have to manage your own fund by yourself. Use the support services available by seeking good advice from your accountant and adviser. Because you have probably already built up a share portfolio you will find that to manage your own super fund will not require much more knowledge. You are already half way there. As I've stated before the super fund will probably cost you in the initial few years but as your fund grows in size you will find that it is one of your best investments.

Don't view your superannuation as your only investment. View it as a bonus to your whole investment portfolio.

16

THE TAX ADVANTAGE

Do not be scared of the taxation laws. The more you understand the tax system the more confident you will become with it. The taxation laws will always be changing and it is your responsibility to understand the changes, or call on your accountant's expertise.

You can utilise the taxation system to your advantage. The tax laws are actually in favour of investing in income-producing assets, as can be seen by the reduction in tax obtained through negative gearing.

CAPITAL GAINS TAX

The Capital Gains Tax (CGT) that was introduced in 1985 is not as damaging as people think it is. Long-term investors, which includes me, are not interested in selling our properties or shares. Therefore capital gains tax will not have to be paid until the investments are sold. Also, we are only likely to sell an investment when we need the money and at this time we are most likely to have a lower taxable income and thus our marginal tax rate will be lower. Therefore the capital gains tax will be minimal. With your own private house you will not be liable to any capital gains tax. Your family home is one of the few remaining tax shelters available to investors.

Study your Capital Gains Tax books and know the Capital Gains Laws. If you have realised gains that are going to be taxed then consider off-setting them with any available capital losses. (This was discussed in detail in Chapter 14.) If you bought an asset after 30 September 1999 and you sell it at least 12 months after the purchase date and make a capital gain, only half of the gain will be subject to tax at your marginal rate. If your marginal rate of tax is at 30 per cent the entire capital gain you make on disposal will be effectively taxed at 15 per cent (plus the Medicare levy).

Say an item was bought on 3 October 1999 for $10,000, then sold on 20 December 2000 for $20,000, the capital gain is $10,000. Fifty per cent of that capital gain is taxable.

$$\$10,000 \times 50\% = \$5000$$

The marginal tax rate is 30 per cent, which means you pay $1500 in tax ($5000 × 30%).

If you hold the item for less than 12 months, the total gain that is made will be taxed at the marginal tax rate for the full gain. Assets that were acquired before 20 September 1985 are excluded from any CGT. If you own any shares or property that were bought before this date and they are appreciating in value, then for tax benefits you may wish to keep them for as long as possible. As long as you hold onto any assets bought on or after 20 September 1985 you will not have to pay any CGT until you sell them.

DIVIDENDS PAID AFTER 30 JUNE 2000

As from 1 July 2000 you will receive a refund for any excess imputation credits. Before this date, if you had any excess credits that were not used up as you had no other tax liability then these credits would be wasted. Therefore you would plan your investments so that you created a large enough taxable income so all of your credits would be used up. You no longer have to worry about this, as any excess credits will be refunded by the Australian Taxation Office. This will be a very big positive for investing in shares, making them more attractive. Of course, legislation is constantly changing, so ask your accountant to advise you of changes as they occur.

FINANCIAL YEAR-END PLANNING

As I have stated a few times in this book earlier, but because of its importance I will state it again, you must do your tax planning before 30 June, so that you can minimise your tax. The best two ways of reducing taxable income are by deferring assessable income until after 30 June or by bringing forward any deductions, so that they are before 30 June. One way to bring a deduction into the present year instead of the next is by paying interest annually in advance on a loan. Or you can contribute more of your taxable income to your superannuation fund.

Many tax sheltering strategies are introduced to the public through advertising, especially during the months of May and June. Do not invest money just because of the tax benefits. You must first look at the possible investment returns and the risks. It is not worth investing into a tax-deductible investment if six months downs the track the investment is worth nothing. The tax benefits of all investing are a bonus and not the reason for investing in the first place. It is far better to pay your tax than to find out later that you have lost all of your invested capital. You should never make an investment decision based purely on tax considerations. You must look at the after-tax return you would expect to receive rather than just looking at ways to reduce your tax.

RENTAL PROPERTY TAX DEDUCTIONS

Most of the tax-deductible rules I have already discussed in chapters 8, 9 and 10. But I need to clarify the situation when you decide soon after buying a property that you are going to repaint the property or put on a carport. These items are not tax-deductible items that would lessen your taxable income for the same year. They are known as Capital Costs. *Not during 1st year*

Your Capital Costs will include any buying and selling costs as well as improvement costs. Your improvement costs and your repair costs are judged to be different for taxation purposes. If you have owned the property for some years and through fair wear and tear you need to repaint it, then you can claim this cost as a tax deductible item in the year that you paint. This is seen as maintenance or repair.

Compare this to the cost of painting the house as soon as you buy the house. This is seen as an improvement and *in 1st year* you cannot claim this cost as a tax-deductible expense in the year that you paint. This cost becomes part of your capital costs so you do not receive the benefits of this capital cost deduction until you sell the property, as it will be subtracted from what your capital gain will be. You cannot claim the costs of improvements immediately but if you use an overdraft facility to pay for the improvements or if you obtain an extension on the initial loan then the interest on this loan is tax deductible.

Capital Gains Tax Example

Purchase House Price	$100,000
Purchase Costs	$5,000
Sale Price	$150,000
Sale Costs	$3,000
Marginal Tax Rate	30%

The week after purchase settlement of the house the whole house was repainted at a cost of $4000. This $4000 is known as a capital cost as it was done to improve the house once purchased. This $4000 is added onto the purchase price.

Purchase House Price	$100,000
Purchase Costs	$5,000
Painting Capital Costs	$4,000
	$109,000
Sale Price	$150,000
Less Sale Costs	$3,000
	$147,000

The Capital Gain is $38,000 ($147,000 – $109,000) and 50 per cent of that gain is taxable. Fifty per cent of this Capital Gain would be $19,000 ($38,000 × 50%) and at a tax rate of 30 per cent you would pay $5700 ($19,000 × 30%) in Capital Gain Tax.

⅙ of profit
or 15%

3.800
19 00
5700

TAX OPPORTUNITIES GONE WRONG

Because of the lack of knowledge, many people buy property and shares in a way that they have not maximised their possible tax deductions. This is one of the biggest errors you can make. People pay cash for their shares and investment properties but will borrow to buy their own private home. The interest on their borrowings cannot be a tax deduction. If they paid cash for their own private home and borrowed to buy the shares or investment property, then the interest on their borrowings would be fully tax deductible.

As an investor you cannot be blamed for not knowing which way to buy assets or which way to use loans. You can be blamed if you have gone and invested without getting your accountant's advice. Don't expect your accountant to get you out of the mess without incurring large costs. Sometimes you won't be able to reverse the situation once it has been executed.

There will nearly always be substantial tax savings if you purchase property and shares correctly. If you do it incorrectly then your tax benefits could be gone forever. This does not apply just for purchases but also for the sale of investments. Again get advice first.

You must not pay more tax than absolutely necessary, which usually occurs because people have not preplanned before executing buy or sell orders. There is no need for the average investor to become the expert in every area of taxation. I leave this to my adviser. Your knowledge, which will increase, and your adviser's knowledge of the way the tax system operates, can be very valuable in achieving tax effectiveness. Never be scared of tax. Find out how the tax rules relate to you and use them to your advantage.

INVESTOR COMPARED WITH EMPLOYEE

An investor has so many more tax advantages that can be used compared to an employee and a self-employed person. The goal of an employee and a self-employed person is to increase their profits but as they do this their tax scenario becomes worse. They work harder and harder and earn more money through working longer hours or by being paid more for their work. Of every extra dollar they make the taxman gets about half.

The aim of the employee and the self-employed person is to have a higher salary and thus a higher taxable income. This is the complete opposite to an investor. An investor wishes to keep his taxable income to a minimum but at the same time he wants to achieve capital growth to a maximum. By keeping his taxable income to a minimum he will pay minimal tax. By keeping his capital growth to a maximum he can use this increased equity as security so that he can buy more investments. These investments again will help decrease his taxable income but increase his total capital gains.

> Employee → Increase Taxable Income →
>   Pays more tax
> Investor → Decrease Taxable Income →
>   Pays Less Tax → Increase Capital Gains

You as an investor must be able to understand the above concept. You must work on increasing your assets and not increasing your taxable income. Any employee or self-employed person can become an investor as well and do exactly the same thing.

> Increase Investments → Increase Assets →
> Borrow Using Assets as Security → Buy
> More Assets → Increase in Capital Gain →
> Borrow More Using Increased Asset Value →
> Repeat.

You must keep on going around as long as you want to. The snowball effect will, to some extent, come into play. Imagine the compounding effect over time now.

Some people will blame their taxes, the economy and the government for their standard of living. Taxes are here for good and will never disappear. None of these concerns are to blame for where you are financially yourself. You can become wealthy in any environment. All you need is the knowledge, which I have given you, and the desire and determination to achieve wealth, which you have to find yourself. Don't sit back and blame the economy for where you are today. It is up to you to achieve what you set out to do.

17

THE CREDIT CARD ADVANTAGE

Australians owe billions of dollars on credit cards. Many people use the credit card to keep their standard of living at the same level. They only pay off the minimum amount each month and as their debt grows over time they realise that they even have trouble finding the money to pay for this minimum amount. At this point some will go out and apply for a larger limit on their cards or obtain another card from a different organisation. Those people are slowly getting themselves into hot water that is about to boil.

Most of these people do not practise delayed gratification. They must have it now. If you are one of these people then you have to realise where it is taking you and rectify the situation immediately. This card is controlling your life.

As employees earn more money they usually find other ways to spend it and banks are more ready to give these people bigger loans or extend their credit card limit to a higher amount. Then they use these credit cards to the limit and thus their interest commitments increase and so they have no money left over by the end of the month.

Having said all that, I have credit cards that have a combined credit limit of over $50,000. But I usually use only one of these cards, which has a limit of $25,000. I always pay off this card so that I do not have to pay interest on it, which is presently at a high rate of about 16 per cent per annum.

There are many advantages to having credit cards, but the big mistake people make is buying depreciating things with their credit cards and not paying off the full amount by the due date. The correct use is to have the availability of a high limit on your credit card and use it only in emergencies or when you know that you are going to pay it out fully by the end of the month.

The reason that I obtain as much as I can on credit card is so that I have extra cash sitting there if I need it in a hurry.

If I found that I needed to contribute $10,000 to my superannuation fund or $10,000 to paying interest in advance on a loan, then I know that I have this money readily available. The reasons for doing this are because of the tax advantages that have been explained previously. But again if I did do this then I would be in a hurry to pay out these cards as quickly as possible. These cash advances on credit cards are for emergencies only.

Every time you are offered a credit card you should accept them for the highest credit limit possible. Most banks will give you a maximum of $10,000 for each card. If you have a partner, then have your partner apply for as many cards as possible as well. Every time you go for a loan also request a credit card and because the bank is already looking over your financials then you won't have to try and prove your reliability again.

From some banks you will be able to get a variety of credit cards. If you have had a credit card for, say, two years and the limit is $2000 then request that the bank extend this limit to the maximum amount. If you have a good track record for paying your minimum repayment off your card every month then the bank is not likely to say no to your request, but they might lift your limit to only $5000 instead of the $10,000. This is still a win situation for you. Your cash flow has just improved if you need the money for an emergency.

PAYING OFF YOUR CARD

It's very seldom that I do not pay out the full amount on my credit card by the time the payment date has arrived. This is because the interest rates on credit cards are very high. So the sooner you have your cards paid out the better. But you should still use the possible 55 days interest-free time available. I pay for everything that I possibly can by card and then pay it out completely on the due date.

On some credit cards you will have to pay about a $30 annual fee, even if you don't use it. This is fine as it is very cheap to pay $30 a year knowing that you have up to $10,000 possible cash immediately if needed. On some cards the annual fee is waived if you spend up to a certain amount within the 12-month period. You have to spend over a certain amount per year to qualify for no fees. Some cards also award loyalty points every time you use them.

Loyalty points are an incentive to buy at any of the stores within the scheme. You accumulate the points and use them for flying, accommodation or to get money vouchers to use. All of these small things can make money or save money. Even though it might only be small, they do add up.

As my father used to say to me: 'It Starts with Just a Penny'.

THE CARD INSTEAD OF A LOAN

Let's assume that the engine on your car has broken down and you need a new engine. You have found out that it will cost you $3000 to fix your car. You haven't the money available but you need the car now so you instruct the mechanic to go ahead and fix it. Where are you going to get the money from?

You can go to the bank and ask for a personal loan. But usually with a personal loan you will have a fairly large establishment fee even though it is for a small amount of money. A personal loan might also have the facility to pay it back over a three-year term. With this scenario you are far better off to use your credit card even though you are paying a higher interest rate. You will not have any establishment cost when you use your credit card. You won't have any penalties for early repayment. Once you use your credit card you now have up to 55 days before you will start paying interest on the loan. But your aim will now be to pay off your credit card first, so hopefully you will only take a few months to pay off your card. Your total interest for this time will be minimal.

Once your card has been paid out you now have this ready-cash available again by having your credit card free of debt. You are now ready for your next emergency.

USE YOUR CARD TO PAY OFF YOUR MORTGAGE

By using your card for purchases that you know you will be able to pay for by the due date, you can save thousands of dollars on your own private home mortgage loan. How does this work?

First of all I have discussed previously that if you have any money on deposit in a bank then you should use this money to pay off part of your loan immediately. You have your card as a backup if you need any funds. Let's assume that you spend $3000 a month on items that you can use your card to pay for. You have up to 55 days before you have to find this $3000 before you incur interest. Therefore you will now budget and save so that you have this $3000 on hand by the due date. This means that your spending will be delayed by about a month so this money can be put into your loan to decrease the principal. Therefore your loan will be paid out over a much shorter time span and thus save you thousands of dollars in interest.

If you become over-committed and have to make a cash withdrawal from your card then you will have to pay interest on this withdrawal from day one. But this will be fine as you will now aim to pay off your card as soon as possible so your high interest rate might only be for one or two months. Naturally if you have not the discipline to pay off your card by the due date then I do not recommend that you use these strategies.

If at present, you find your card is causing you a lot of concern then give it to a friend to put it away for you until you pay it out completely. Then once you have learned sensible money habits you can start to introduce it slowly.

You must have control of your card. Most people have their card controlling them. What category do you fall under?

THE COSTS OF A CREDIT CARD

One of the biggest wealth creation tragedies is that some people will use credit cards for all of the wrong reasons. Some people will obtain two or more cards and then just keep on spending on things that have very little value once they have been bought. These people have the 'Need It Now' mentality. If only they realised what these cards, when used wrongly, will do to them.

On the cards that they own, assume that they have a combined credit limit of $30,000. The interest rate on these cards will be about 16 per cent. That's a total of $4800 interest in a year ($30,000 × 16%). This equals $400 a month interest payments on $30,000 worth of items that would sell for a total of about $5000 if you could sell them.

Look at the opportunity costs that these credit cards have produced. If you bought two investment homes and rented them out you would find that your own cash flow to service these loans would be about $400 a month. Throughout this book I have shown you how to calculate this. Your capital gain on these houses could be up to $30,000 a year or even more. So therefore the $30,000 that you have spent using your card is costing you around $30,000 a year in lost profit. And as seen with the compounding effect of money over time, this $30,000 would increase every year.

Also, as the equity in these two properties increased by

$30,000 a year you could continually buy more properties over the years or create a very large share portfolio. How much has your credit card cost you in the past? What are you going to do about it?

18

CONTROL YOUR OWN RISK

'But that is too risky.'

'But no it's not.'

It is amazing how the word invest immediately brings to mind the word risk. Let me repeat something that I have already stated in this book. I am a very conservative investor and I am not interested at all in taking any great risks. You must understand my views about taking risks and this is how I have always been.

I minimise my risks always and that is done by having control of my risk level at all times. I manage my own risk. You will not be able to avoid some risk but you can control your level of risk. You must 'play it smart' rather than, 'play it too safe'.

Every day you put yourselves at risk and you always work at minimising this risk. You wear a seat belt in a car because you know that you lessen the risk. You obtain insurance on your house and your car so you do not risk losing money if something happens to them. Investments should be treated the exact same way. No matter what happens to my investments I know that I have no risk of losing my money. I look for insurance on my investments just like I have insurance on my car.

CALCULATE YOUR RISK

How much money did you risk in buying this book? You would have calculated that before you paid your money. If you didn't then you must start doing it. Before you spend any money see if you are going to receive your money's worth for it. You are risking your money.

This money's worth that I am talking about can come in different forms. Money to buy food satisfies the appetite. Money to see a film will give entertainment and learning experiences. Money to buy the heater will give warmth on cold wintry days. Money to buy this book will give you financial rewards. It will give you education, it will give you motivation and it might even make you smile every now and then. What you get out of this book and what someone else gets out of this book could be completely different. The risk that you have taken in buying this book is that you will get nothing out of it at all.

You must sum up the risks of every investment in the same way, before you buy them. I could go and buy many more shares today with the available money that I have but then my risks would increase. I am not interested in increasing these risks. Let's assume that I am to receive a cheque this afternoon for over $100,000 which I could use to obtain another $200,000 through margin lending and buy $300,000 worth of shares.

$100,000	Cheque to be received today
$200,000	Using margin lending
$300,000	Purchase of Shares

But I will not do this as I calculate that there is too much of a risk.

Loan money = $200,000 ÷ Valuation = $300,000 = 66%
66% loan/value ratio is far too high for me.

I will park this money in my account until I find the best place to put it. I can even pay off some of my margin lending loan with it so that I will no longer be charged interest on this margin loan. Then when I see another opportunity to buy I can withdraw this money immediately to use it.

I am minimising my risks by not over gearing to a loan/value ratio of 66 per cent and I am doing my homework on my next investment. I am not in a hurry to invest my money. I am giving myself a lot of time to think. This is your best way to minimise risk.

SEIZE OPPORTUNITIES

How much money would you 'risk' to buy the secrets of becoming a millionaire? I want you to put a figure on it. Don't forget what sort of lifestyle you could have if you were a millionaire. What are your specific figures? $10, $20, $100, or $1000? It can be any amount you like.

If you really believe that you can become a millionaire, by knowing how to become a millionaire and having the true desire to become a millionaire then what amount of money would you invest to do this? Reread the above section and think about it seriously because the way you answer this question will have a very strong bearing on whether you will succeed or not. Try to work out for yourself what I am saying to you here.

THERE IS ALWAYS RISK

There will always be some amount of risk that things will go against you. You might lose your job tomorrow. Now that is a very big risk to some people. For some people they would not be able to cope but for others it might be a positive. Look at where it could lead you.

Many people waste a lot of time waiting for everything to be perfect and to fall into place before they get anything done. You must act now. There is never a time when everything is perfect. There will be never a time when there will be no risk at all. People that won't take any risks will never get anywhere.

I'm not saying don't cover your own back. What I am saying is that you should recognise the risks, manage the risks by partially minimising them, and then if everything stacks up correctly you take action. Don't be too cautious or it will cause you to miss out on a lot of great opportunities. I am not just talking about financial opportunities here. I am talking about all opportunities in life.

As I have shown you in some examples throughout this book, it is possible to achieve high returns on your money while maintaining low risk. As long as you absorb the knowledge you will be able to do it quite easily. These are not 'secret ways'. The information is out there. You just have to know where to find it. Now you can learn many of these so-called 'secrets' by studying this book.

You do not minimise your risk by keeping all of your money in a bank deposit account. In this case you are losing the value of your money because of inflation and tax. At first you will make some mistakes and that is why I recommend that you begin investing slowly. Do not rush into it with all of your available money. Invest initially with a small amount of money. As you become more accustomed to investing you will know what you are looking for. Don't avoid the risk but instead learn how to manage the risk.

You will often hear people say that, 'You must learn from your mistakes'. I think it is far better and a lot cheaper to, 'Learn from other people's mistakes'. Now is the time to take responsibility for yourself.

'It will be all right. The government will look after me.' How many people do you know that have this attitude? If they lose their job they can apply for unemployment benefits. Once their superannuation runs out they can rely on the pension. These people are taking a far greater risk than those who are investing. Could you live on the pension? Could you live on less than $160 a week?

It is riskier to not invest than it is to invest. I do not promote that you expose yourself to unacceptable risks. What I do promote is that you quantify the risk before you make a move and not afterwards. You will start to know how much risk you are willing to take. If something is calculated to have too much risk then you must step back and find ways to minimise the risk before you step forward again. The more you study the scenario the less risk you will allow.

WE ALL VIEW RISK DIFFERENTLY

Most entrepreneurs do not take on a lot of risk and will usually have the odds stacked in their favour. What you might see as being risky will not be risky to the entrepreneur because they have educated themselves about the investment. Some people will comment that they think that I am doing something very risky, where I do not see any risk at all. I do not set out to take risks but instead I set out to minimise risks. Many people will have the perception that there is too greater risk and therefore will be scared of doing anything. The fear of losing money is often a lot stronger than the belief of making money. So some risks must be taken. The person who risks nothing, does nothing and has nothing.

There is no such thing as risk-free investments. Always be willing to take some risks, but manage these risks to a minimum. I have discussed in many areas how to manage the main three risks of investing.

1. Buy the right shares or properties.
2. Obtain the correct loans.
3. Never, never, never, over-extend yourself by buying too much and/or borrowing too much.

Taking out the correct insurances is also one of the best ways to reduce your risks.

THE IMPORTANCE OF INSURANCE

Insurance is such a big topic that you could write a whole book about it and there probably already are fairly extensive books and pamphlets that have been published that will inform you of everything that you need to know. I will list the different types of insurances that Mary and I have to give you an understanding of what insurances we believe are essential.

If you can, you must find an insurance broker who you can trust. Ask around and find out who other people use. Every time insurance comes due make sure you are fully covered for the next 12 months. You would be in a very risky position if the car is stolen or the unit burns down, if you don't have the correct insurance.

Insure Yourself   The most important insurance, I believe, is to insure yourself. From the time that we started to invest and therefore started to obtain some fairly substantial loans we realised that the money that was required to service these loans came from the active work that Mary and I did at the time. If one of us could not work for whatever reason then our cash flow would be diminished substantially and it would be so much harder to service the loans.

There were two possibilities where one wage would disappear. One of us could become sick or injured and so we would not be able to work, or one of us could die. We had to consider both possibilities and insure ourselves in case this did ever happen.

While you are working for someone else you might have sickness benefits available but what happens when these benefits run out? You will require sickness and accident insurance, which will usually have a waiting period of about two weeks from the time that you have stopped work before you will receive any benefits. During these two weeks you are still likely to receive some income, as you will most likely have accrued some sick leave for which you will be paid.

If you are self-employed then you will not have any sick leave available so you must have insurance to cover this possibility. You might decide to cover yourself with a policy that will start paying you once you have been off work for two weeks and it will pay you $500 a week for the next two years or until you return to work. This is exactly what Mary and I had while we were in business. Once our assets had grown substantially we did not continue with this insurance.

You will find that there are so many different policies available that will pay you different amounts for different periods of time. This is where you have to do your own homework well and work out exactly what you want to be covered for. You must read all of the policy on offer and see if it is exactly what you want. This applies to all insurances.

Inform the insurance agency what you are looking for and they will usually be able to put a policy together to suit your needs. So many people will not get around to putting a policy together to insure themselves even though they will definitely insure their house and their car. Again, what we are doing here is minimising risk. People do not expect to lose the ability to work themselves. A prolonged time without work can have a drastic effect on a family's standard of living. How long could you last without one income coming into your household? You still have all of the same expenses to cover except for maybe a few. Would your standard of living diminish dramatically?

Your health is one of your best assets. A person with bad health problems can lose a lot of self-esteem. If you had money problems once you could not work this would make the situation even worse. Make sure you have guaranteed renewable income protection insurance. Therefore if you were to fall ill then the insurance company cannot cancel your policy. They must renew it the following year. If you unfortunately have to claim income protection insurance then it will be at about 75 per cent of what your normal income was. The reason that the insurance company is not likely to cover you for 100 per cent of your income is because you then have no incentive in going back to work. If you wanted cover over the 75 per cent then the premium is likely to increase dramatically.

Term Insurance   Mary and I also took out Term Insurance and Death and Disability Insurance. These insurances we took out in our superannuation as there were better tax advantages by doing it this way. One policy, which we both have, covers each one of us if either of us die, for whatever reason. A large sum of money will be paid out to the surviving partner. Initially, we put a figure on this amount which was equal to the amount of debt that we had in total. So therefore if one of us died the insurance policy would pay out all of our debts and so the income coming in from the investments in the shares and property would not have to be used to service any loans. It could be used to live on. To obtain this Term Insurance we paid a premium at the beginning of the year that would have to be paid each year on its anniversary. It was just like paying the car insurance. At the end of the year we had to repay the premium. As our assets grew more we took out another Term Insurance for both Death and Disability.

If you haven't enough investments to provide an adequate cash flow for the surviving partner then you will need to take out a much larger insurance amount which will then be invested to provide an income stream. A surviving family with only the private house as an asset will definitely need a large payout from insurance to allow for an adequate lifestyle.

A single person might not require term insurance but when you have a partner and family who depend on your income then both adults definitely need it. You could have the situation where the wife does not work and so you wonder what are the advantages of her life being insured as well. If she died and you had children you might want to stay home with the children and therefore you need some income from elsewhere. Or, your choice might be to have the family cared for which again will cost a lot of money. By covering yourself you are minimising your risks.

When you insure, for whatever reason, make sure you ask questions if anything in the policy is unclear. You will have a right to change your mind with a cooling off period of 14 days. If you want to withdraw from the policy then exercise this right. Don't under-insure yourself or your property. It will not cost a lot more to increase your insurance so don't worry about this little extra cost. You are lessening your risk.

Car Insurance   I always make sure that my cars are well insured. I have had a new car stolen so this might have something to do with this. This car was about 15 months old when it was stolen and has never been recovered. I had paid the renewal notice when I had had the car for 12 months but I should have insured it for an 'agreed value' and not the 'market value'. The car had only done about 25,000 kilometres and was kept like new. The payout figure, which was their 'market value', was $48,800. To buy another new one at the time was about $59,000. I figured mine was worth about $53,000 so whatever way you look at it I lost money.

After this happened I would ring each year to find out what was the maximum agreed value I could put on each car and would insure for that amount. The premium was always a little bit more but at least I knew I would receive the full amount of the agreed value back if there was a need again. Look around for the best price when it comes to any insurances but especially cars.

With one of my cars, I insured it with the condition that no one under the age of 30 would drive it and that there was an excess of $1000 if Mary or I did not drive it at the time of an accident. By putting these conditions in, the policy cost me over $300 less. It also gives me a good excuse to say no to any friends who wanted to have a drive. I would tell them that I couldn't allow them to drive it, as it wouldn't be insured.

Even if your car is only worth a few thousand dollars it is still worth insuring it for an agreed value. If you didn't insure it for say $4000 and then it was damaged, well

$4000 is still a lot to lose. You must always have insurance that will protect the property or car that you could damage with your own car.

House Contents Insurance   You should spend a few hours going from room to room in your house and writing down everything that you own that is in the house. You will be amazed what it would cost to replace the objects that you have in the house at present. You must add up everything from your fridge to your cutlery. It has all cost you money and if you have a fire in the house then it will cost you a lot of money to buy everything again. Your contents might add up to $50,000, $70,000 or even more. Don't under-insure yourself. You have to work out a reasonable value for all of these items and insure yourself for that amount.

You must recheck this amount each year and make sure that you increase the cover if there is a need. Your house will be increasing in value as well so make sure that you slightly over-insure your house to allow for the price increase of your house over the next 12-month period. Never under-insure, as there are penalties for doing so that can cost you a lot of money if you have to make a claim.

The Unit Is On Fire! It is one o'clock in the morning on Easter Monday and I am having a cuppa just before going to bed. I'm startled by the phone ringing, especially when the only noise at that time of morning was the humming of the fridge. Something was wrong. No one rings at this time; not usually anyway.

I answered the phone. In a very softly spoken voice a voice says, 'Sean your unit is on fire and the fire trucks have just arrived'. I drove over to the unit and it was completely burnt out. The police and the fire brigade said it looked like an electric blanket had caused the fire. The tenants were away on holidays. I rang the builder who had built the units for us and he came around and secured the house, or what was left of it.

I was home asleep by about three in the morning. I did not have to worry about anything. The unit was insured which also covered the rent that I would lose while it was being rebuilt. The following morning the C.I.B. was called in and asked me to assist with their questions. This was another story. It was established that the fire had been deliberately lit. The next day the insurance company met me and rebuilding commenced within one week. The cost to the insurance company was about $64,000. The cost to us was Mary's time in picking curtains, carpet, paint etc. Make sure you are fully insured. The bank would not have been impressed if I wasn't.

Power of Attorney Who has power of attorney over you? If you became ill and could not sign your name then who can sign your name for you. Make sure you have Power of Attorney over your wife and vice versa. I also have two other people who have Power of Attorney over us, just in case we were both involved in an accident.

It is best that you seek legal advice concerning this and at the same time make sure that your wills are up to date. If you have not read your own will in the last six months then get it out immediately and read it slowly. Do not read any more of this book until you have read your will. You should revise your will every year and discuss it with your partner.

Circumstances often change and thus you need to review the direction of your will. Discuss your will with your financial adviser and also with your solicitor. They might see ways in which it will be more beneficial for your assets to be distributed. This also is true for your insurance broker. He will see better ways for you to insure yourself. This is his job.

CONCLUSION – IT ALL STARTED
WITH A DREAM

My dreams and your dreams will be very different. And the word 'dream' might be hard to grasp at first but don't let a little word stop you from getting to where you deserve to go. A child starts with a dream. A teenager has his or her own dream. A married couple has their own dreams. A 40-year-old single person has his own dream. What Is Your Dream? What is Your Goal?

Are you willing to work hard enough and smart enough to achieve your dreams? Can you, along with a lot of help from many other people, reach your dreams? Of course you can. It is entirely in your control.

You have come a long way since you picked up this book and believe me this is only the beginning. I have probably tested and stretched many of your beliefs. Many of the ideas that I have introduced to you will be very scary. You must now set your own goals from today. Write them down and be proud of them. You must put a given time down for each one of your goals.

I will give you an example of what your financial goals might be so that you can be guided by them and thus establish your own goals. Don't forget your goals can change often and your time limits can also change. This does not matter. What does matter is that you have all of your goals written down with a date next to them.

SET YOUR FINANCIAL GOALS

In exactly the same way as I have set my goals you need to set your goals for your financial freedom. Your goals might be completely different and that is great. You must know what you want yourself and then work toward it. Don't concern yourself with what other people want, and don't let other people tell you what you should want.

This goal setting exercise is an example only and I want you to use it to your advantage in any way you want to. I will number the goals but they do not have to be in any particular order.

1. I will pay out my credit cards within two months from today. Put down an exact date and work out how much you must pay off per day. Assume your present balance is $3400. How much do you have to pay out each day? $55.74 ($3400 ÷ 61 days).
2. I will then save $40 a day and put it into a bank account every Monday and Thursday. Five days a week × $40 × 52 weeks = $10,400 in my first year.
3. In two years time from today I will buy my first investment property. Note down the date.
4. I will have $500,000 worth of gross assets within four years from today.

5. I will have over $700,000 worth of net assets within nine years from today.
6. I will have over $900,000 worth of net assets within 11 years from today.
7. I will have reached the $1,000,000 mark in the 13th year from today. About half of these assets will be shares and the other half will be properties. On the day that I reach this figure I will put in an order for the car of my dreams.

You must reward yourself as you achieve different levels of your goals. This is very important. You might find the above examples too aggressive for yourself or you might look at them and see that you are already well on your way. Every person will be at a different level.

KNOW WHERE YOU ARE GOING

Once you have set your goals you know where you are going. Nothing will stop you. You know how long it will take to get there. If you don't know where you are going to then how will you know where to start? Yet, if you know where you are going then you are already halfway there.

Most people will not set financial goals. They do not know where they are going. Their lives are in neutral. They are very comfortable drifting along with the rest of the mob. If your desire is to become financially independent then your goal must be clear-cut and well defined. You must put an exact monetary figure on financial freedom. If you only have a vague figure on financial freedom then you are not as likely to get there.

Also you might have all the books and tapes required to learn about becoming financially free but if you are not prepared to travel along the road then you will never get to your destination. You must be willing to do the required work.

You also must look ahead. Where do you want to be in 10 years time? Look ahead 10 years and imagine what sort of person you will be. You must set your goals for 10 years down the track. It is just like me writing the book. Looking back it has been relatively easy. If you don't set your goals for 10 years down the track then you will not grow in that direction. Before you start on the next 10-year journey know where you want to go.

In 10 years time what sort of standard of living would you like to achieve? To have this standard of living what sort of assets will you have to have? To achieve the ownership of these assets in 10 years time how much do you have to have in two years time and in four years time? Set an exact value for every year. This is your journey. This is the road you must take.

Investing In Your Physical Well-being How fit are you? When was the last time you did 30 minutes of endurance work? Most people are finding that their lives are becoming more hectic every year and they find it hard to have any time to look after their physical well-being.

You don't want to be the richest man in the graveyard. Are you going to run down the beach when you retire or are you going to hobble down the beach?

Some people will exercise more than they did say five years ago but you read how one in three people do not exercise at all, and that over 12 per cent of the population have high blood pressure. Are you a person who does no exercise at all or a person who has high blood pressure? Are you going to put all of these hours into building up your wealth but then find that you are not healthy enough to enjoy it?

Goal setting is relevant to your physical well-being.

If you want a bit of thinking time about a specific problem, do you decide to go for a walk so you have time to think about it or do you decide to have a couple of wines? Which is better for you? If you feel better physically on any given day then you are more likely to be more productive. You will have the energy to get more things done. Daily exercise is an outstanding motivation tool. You can do a lot of thinking while you are running or swimming or you can just let your mind relax and forget about everything else. Both situations are extremely beneficial.

Put your health first. No matter how much money you have, if you haven't good health then the money isn't worth having.

TELL YOUR GOALS TO YOUR ADVISER

If your adviser is not interested in what your short-term, medium-term, and long-term financial goals are then he is not for you. Your adviser must know what your goals are and respect your decision and desire to achieve these goals.

He cannot help you achieve your financial goals if he doesn't believe that you can achieve them yourself. This is why you should have your goals written down and present them to your adviser. He will then know what path you are taking and see how aggressive you are.

The people you love the most, your family, must know what your goals are. By discussing your goals with your partner they will become combined goals and then you already have someone who is backing you all of the way. You are setting your goals for the benefit of your family.

HOW DO WE SET OUR FINANCIAL GOALS?

1. For your goal to become financially free you must set an exact amount of money that will indicate that you are now financially free. This amount of money might be $2,000,000. You must be convinced that the $2,000,000 will give you financial freedom.

2. You will not succeed in achieving your goal unless you are willing to give something in return for your goal. You will not be able to obtain 'something for nothing'.

3. You must create a definite plan on how you are going to achieve your goals. This will look similar to the example I have given in this chapter but in far more detail. You must start today. Not tomorrow or when everything is just right. It doesn't work that way. You will start this minute. Actually you have already started.

4. For every long-term, medium-term, and short-term goal you will establish a definite date. You will know exactly what money you will possess at each one of these dates.

5. This is one of the most important things to do. You must read your goals as described in the first four points at least once every day. As I have said, when I was explaining about Self-Talk, you must read your goals out aloud. As you are doing this you must allow your imagination and emotion free run. You must already believe that you have achieved your goals. The money is already yours.

It is so important that you see the need for doing the above five procedures. Follow the system. Do what works and your belief will continually become stronger. If you wish to become financially free then you must first dream a lot. You will imagine what it will be like. You will keep on wishing and as your desires become stronger you will begin to plan. You will do the above procedure and you have already begun this journey of becoming financially free.

Most people will achieve their goals the minute they write their goals down. Many people will become rich as soon as they set themselves a dollar value and a date that they will achieve it. You must know exactly where you are heading or the chances of getting there are very slim. If instead of writing down the magical figure and the date that you would have reached it, you just kept it in your head, then your goal will become very vague. You can change the amount and date at any time. You have nothing concrete written down.

Most people will not establish a dollar value or a date. Their thinking is, 'I'm going to be rich'. Ask somebody what their net worth will be in 10 years time from now. See what sort of answer you receive. Most people will not have a clue. Their answer might be 'Well, it will depend on my salary at the time'. You need to be so much more exact that this.

Let me now ask you; how much in net assets will you have in 10 years time from today? Can you answer this question? If you can't then reread this chapter immediately. Let me ask you another question.

In one year from today what will be your weekly income and what will be the value of your net assets? Write it down at the bottom of this page and put the date of one year from today. As you pick this book up from time to time in the future you will be able to refer back to this page and see how you are travelling.

I recommend that you write down the exact amount of net assets you will have for the next 10 years. Put the date including the year next to every amount. Don't be scared. Let your imagination run, as your imagination will become reality if you really want it to.

It might be a good idea at this point to go for a walk by yourself and do a lot of dreaming, thinking, calculating, goal setting. Call it whatever you want to. Don't forget that one of your biggest assets is your ability to think. If you haven't got a dream then how are you going to make your dreams come true? Visualise why you want to become financially free. You must be able to see it out there in front of you. If you had the time and financial resources, what would you do with your life? What would you be doing now?

FURTHER RESOURCES

A Better Way to Live, Og Mandino (Bantam Books, New York, 1990).

Building Wealth in Changing Times, Jan Somers (Somerset Financial Services Pty Ltd, Queensland, 1994).

Building Wealth Story by Story, Jan Somers (Somerset Financial Services Pty Ltd, Queensland, 1998).

Building Wealth Through Investment Property, Jan Somers (Somerset Financial Services Pty Ltd, Queensland, 1992).

Cash Flow Quadrant, Robert Kiyosaki (TechPress Inc., Arizona, 1998).

The E-Myth, Michael Gerber (HarperCollins Publishers Inc., New York, 1995).

How to Buy Shares Cheap and Make Big Profits, Chris Tate (Information Australia, Melbourne, 1993).

How to Double Your Profits Within the Year, John Fenton (Pan Books Ltd, London, 1981).

How to Start With No Savings and Get Rich Safely, Stuart Moore (Hudson Institute, Queensland, 1991).

How to Win Friends and Influence People, Dale Carnegie (Pocket Books, New York, 1981).

If You Want to Be Rich and Happy Don't Go to School, Robert Kiyosaki (Aslan Publishing, Connecticut, 1992).

The Investors Quotient, Jake Bernstein (John Wiley & Sons Inc., New York, 1993).

Making Money Made Simple, Noel Whittaker (Simon & Schuster, Sydney, 1992).

Rich Dad, Poor Dad, Robert Kiyosaki (TechPress Inc., Arizona, 1997).

The Richest Man in Babylon, George Clason (Penguin Books, New York, 1991).

Rupert Murdoch, Jerome Tuccille (Donald I. Fine Inc., New York, 1989).

The 7 Habits of Highly Effective People, Stephen Covey (Simon & Schuster, New York, 1989).

The Warren Buffett Way, Robert G. Hagstrom Jr. (John Wiley & Sons Inc., New York, 1995).

Think and Grow Rich, Napoleon Hill (Ballantine Books, New York, 1960).

Your Mortgage and How to Pay it Off in Five Years, Anita Bell (Random House Australia Pty Ltd, Sydney, 1999).

201 Tax and Investment Strategies, Daryl Dixon (Information Australia, Melbourne, 1991).

AUDIO TAPES

Awaken the Giant Within, Anthony Robbins (Simon & Schuster, New York, 1991).

The First Day of the Rest of Your Life, Zig Ziglar (The Seminar Company, Queensland, 1993).

How to Break Bad Habits, Denis Waitley (The Seminar Company, Queensland, 1993).

Making Money Machine, Winston Marsh (Winston Marsh Pty Ltd, Victoria, 1993).

Mega Memory, Kevin Trudeau (Nightingale Conant, Illinois, 1991).

Mega Speed Reading, Howard Stephen Berg (TRU-Vantage International, USA, 1996).

Millionaire Magic, James Rohn (The Seminar Company, Queensland, 1993).

Million Dollars Secrets, Denis Waitley (The Seminar Company, Queensland, 1993).

Power Talk, Anthony Robbins (Vision Publishing, Sydney, 1996).

Psychocybernetics, Maxwell Malts (The Seminar Company, Queensland, 1993).

Top Performance, Zig Ziglar (The Training Company, Texas, 1988).

YOUR JOURNEY TO FINANCIAL FREEDOM
HAS ALREADY BEGUN!

I'm planning to write more material in the future. If you want to know when this material will become available, or if you have any comments or questions about this book, please write to me at the following address:

Sean O'Reilly
PO Box 1335
Warragul
VICTORIA 3820